D0906290

NOT PEACE
BUT
A SWORD

By Vance Havner

BY THE STILL WATERS
THE SECRET OF CHRISTIAN JOY
ROAD TO REVIVAL
REST AWHILE
IT IS TIME!
HEARTS AFIRE
DAY BY DAY
REST FOR THE WEARY
REPENT OR ELSE!
TRUTH FOR EACH DAY
PEACE IN THE VALLEY
WHY NOT JUST BE CHRISTIANS?
PEPPER 'N SALT
LIVING IN KINGDOM COME
IT IS TOWARD EVENING
JESUS ONLY
IN TIMES LIKE THESE
SEASONINGS
NOT PEACE BUT A SWORD

NOT PEACE
BUT
A SWORD

VANCE HAVNER

FLEMING H. REVELL COMPANY
Old Tappan, New Jersey

Scripture references in this volume are from the *King James Version of the Bible.*

"The Old Rugged Cross" by George Bennard, Words and Music Copyright, The Rodeheaver Co., Owner, Used by Permission.

"I Have Decided to Follow Jesus," Copyright 1949 by Zondervan Music Publishers. All rights reserved. Used by permission.

SBN 8007–0470–3

Copyright © 1971 by Fleming H. Revell Company
All Rights Reserved
Library of Congress Catalog Card Number: 76–160274
Printed in the United States of America

To all comrades who are committed to the Way
that means *not peace but a sword.*

CONTENTS

8

PREFACE

This is not a novel in the modern sense. It is only an effort to use a different medium to set forth some convictions. It has seemed to me that putting them in the format of a city pastor writing his own experiences might make it more personal.

I have put together here a sort of mosaic gathered from over half a century of preaching in local churches all over America. Some of these experiences have happened in varied application, and all could happen if and when at least some in any congregation follow a dedicated leader in taking Jesus Christ seriously.

Some who produce books on how to write may find faults in this account, but I have written for grass-roots people who will manage to eat the meat and not choke on the bones. Those who travel the way which is *not peace but a sword* will get the message.

VANCE HAVNER

NOT PEACE
BUT
A SWORD

1
STEPHEN LYNN

I should have been happy in Memorial Church. It was my first pastorate out of seminary and one of the top ten charges in the state. I had my doctorate, my travel abroad, and was a member of two important boards. (An old-school evangelist, with Paul's shipwreck en route to Rome in mind, used to say, "If you can't swim, get on a board!") I was well fixed and Uncle Bill Blaine, who wasn't too careful with his figures of speech, said, "Reverend, if you play your hand well, you've got it made."

Memorial was *the* church of Riverby—imposing and important. A liberal sprinkling of lawyers, doctors, merchants, and politicians sat in the pews—on Sunday mornings, that is. We were definitely *in*. Everything was peaceful for nobody was likely to get excited enough about religion to start a commotion. The only spot in Riverby that was more tranquil was Valley View Cemetery. (There were other similarities!)

But I couldn't shake off a haunting dissatisfaction with the status quo. At seminary we aspiring young Timothys sat up late many a night talking about what would happen if somebody should resolve to be: just a Christian. What if one should set out—free from all the trappings, the accumulations, the traditions, the Establishment—to recover the elemental simplicity of first-century Christianity? I had read *In*

His Steps years before, and although it certainly had no
literary excellence, the fact that eight million copies had been
sold and that it is still being read certainly indicated something. We seminary upstarts never settled anything in our
discussions, but the theme was intriguing and I still had
spells pondering it amidst the modern complexities of
Memorial Church.

What a commentary on modern Christianity—that after
twenty centuries of it we should be wondering what would
happen if we started out to take Jesus Christ seriously!
Shouldn't we have been doing just that all the time? What
are churches for? Why should it be sensational today to be
really a Christian? Shouldn't the exception be the rule? Why
should it be unusual when it was meant to be the norm? Alas,
we are so subnormal that to be normal would be counted
abnormal!

I suppose I would have gone on mulling over the matter
in uneasy moments—but never doing much about it—if Stephen Lynn had not come to Riverby. My church visitor had
discovered him and reported him to me. I went to see him
in his bachelor apartment over by the river. I found him to
be very pleasant, but not disposed to talk about himself. Any
individual who does not like to talk about himself is a rarity
to begin with! When I saw that he was not inclined to give
much personal information, I switched to other topics and
found that he opened up when we got around to spiritual
matters. He had no theological training, but was well read,
and knew how to handle his much-used Bible. When we
talked about this matter of taking Christ seriously Stephen
Lynn glowed. It was contagious. He opined that too much
of our Christianity is secondhand. It is like eating canned
goods instead of vegetables from your own garden.

"I want to be a first-hander," he said. Lynn lamented that we seem more interested in perpetuating an institution than in reproducing an experience, and quoted Dr. J.B. Phillips' words about Christianity beginning as an experience, but becoming a performance. He was not antichurch, but spoke of "the church within the church," the fellowship of true believers everywhere. Organization and system and the Establishment are means to an end, but when they become ends in themselves, God starts over with a new fellowship. We are seeing this in underground movements, Lynn said, in prayer and Bible study groups, extracurricular activities. Some are wild and way-out, but the false implies the true. God raises up the irregular to revive the regular. These things come and go but the church rolls on. (These were some of this surprising man's ideas.)

Of course I knew all this already but while I viewed it academically from the security of my salaried pastorate, Stephen Lynn was really out to give it a try. He said we needed people who would simply trust Jesus for everything and see what would happen. I was convinced that for Stephen Lynn something would happen soon!

Rumors began to get around that a stranger was approaching various individuals to discuss their spiritual needs. Stephen Lynn talked to men at work, called on offices, visited homes, conversed with others on the streets. He had nothing to sell, no organization to join. His subject was Jesus Christ —and since he was peddling nothing—it threw his listeners off guard. There was nothing professional about it for he was perfectly natural. Nobody told him to attend to his business for this seemed to be his business. There was nothing bookish about it, as though he had taken a course in personal witness-

ing with chapters on how to deal with different cases. It
wasn't bearing witness so much as just *being* a witness.

After he had been in Riverby some weeks Lynn started a
little prayer meeting and Bible study in his apartment. ("The
early church started in homes, you know."),Ten came the
first time, then they filled his living room and from there they
moved to a room at the Y. Two of my flock were in on it from
the start: Linwood Sanders, a good Christian who always
liked such gatherings, and Sarah Lott, wife of Howson Lott,
real estate man and a hardened old sinner. She had prayed
for Howson for years and seized every opportunity for such
prayer as a drowning man grabs a straw.

Curiosity got the best of me and I attended one of Lynn's
meetings. They sang a few songs and he gave a brief Bible
message. Then they prayed. There was nothing strange or
unusual except that old-fashioned prayer meetings are
strange and unusual! The report had started that Lynn was
a member of an off-beat sect. And of course there was the
suspicion that he was starting a new church. He stopped that
by advising converts to join some church where the Bible is
believed and taught. Actually, he was starting a new "church
within the church" by seeking to stir up a fellowship of
Christians who would infiltrate all their churches with a new
experience and a fresh testimony of vital original Christianity. He warned the group severely against becoming mere
troublemakers in their churches. He said there are two kinds
of division mentioned in the New Testament: division on
account of Christ (John 7:43; 9:16; 10:19) and divisions on
account of false teachers (Romans 16:17). He said everything
depended on whether the division was on account of *Him* or
them!

Lynn made it very clear, however, that Jesus did not come

to earth to bring peace but a sword, and that loyalty to Him
would divide families (Matthew 10:34–39; Luke 12:49–53).
He said we were long on membership and short on discipleship these days in our churches, and that following Christ
was the costliest business on earth, but paid greatest rewards.
He scored cheap Christianity that would accept Jesus as
Saviour—but refuse to confess Him as Lord. He said salvation was free but that it cost Christ everything to provide it
and would cost us everything to possess it. (I can see how this
would jar the average congregation to whom joining church
is merely the accepted thing to do—a status symbol that will
look good in an obituary someday!)

Stephen Lynn closed his meeting with prayer. Everybody
prayed from the heart. What a contrast to the pitiful sentence
prayers on Wednesday night at Memorial! How we try to
pull out of hearts what is not in them! ("What is down in the
well will come up in the bucket," but, alas, so many wells are
dry.)

I came away from that meeting with the words of our
Lord, *I came not to send peace but a sword,* burned into my
heart. Would I dare to really trust Him for everything and
see what happens? Was I afraid of the sword?

2
HOWSON LOTT

Stephen Lynn was not interested in building a mutual congratulation society. He urged his group to prove their sincerity by going after their friends and neighbors. Many had already done that when I visited the meeting. Several had been converted and had joined different churches. The salt began to permeate. After all, salt never did any good in a salt shaker and I have worried about our million-dollar salt cellars on street corners where Christians come to sit but never go out to serve.

Eventually four new Christians from Lynn's fellowship came to join Memorial Church. There were some lifted eyebrows when they came forward for baptism as though some doubtful foreigners were invading our premises. There was some low-key criticism, but I observed that these four were four more than any of the critics had won to Christ to my knowledge while I had been in Riverby! Most of our additions have come from the Junior Department in Sunday school, or lettered-in folk from other churches. Four brand-new grown-up converts are rarities in Memorial Church. Two of the four had been church members but had never been Christians. Could that have made some of our people a little uneasy within? I'd hate to know how many of our membership need to be converted and baptized—not rebap-

tized—because if they have never been Christians they have
never been scripturally baptized. Too many are what they
have always been, and anyone who is what he has always
been is not a Christian!

Not peace but a sword became a living reality in Riverby
before Stephen Lynn had been here six months. He told me
privately that he had no intention of staying in our city, but
would move on to start a similar movement somewhere else.
He was not building something around himself. What had
been begun must continue without his leadership, growing
by the daily witness of a Master's minority who would infiltrate—not just the churches—but the whole life of Riverby
by their life and testimony.

It was not long before we saw the flash of the sword in
Memorial Church. At one of our deacons' meetings, Jeffrey
Fullerton, chairman of our board, blasted the new movement
in caustic terms. He labeled it a wild-fire excitement that
would feed extremists into our churches, upsetting some
good people, and destroying the peace and harmony of our
religious life in Riverby. (Bethel might have made the same
complaint about Amos and Pharisaism about our Lord!)
Fullerton would have no part in it and thought we should nip
it in the bud.

But the bud was already in bloom and the blossom that
created most upheaval was none other than Howson Lott
himself when he walked down the aisle to make a profession
of faith. I don't believe the congregation would have looked
more stunned if I had dropped dead in the pulpit. Howson
had gone to one of Lynn's prayer meetings at his wife's
insistence. Lynn had visited him in his office and home. It
was a new Howson Lott who joined Memorial Church that
Sunday. One such convert is worth a thousand arguments.

*And beholding the man which was healed . . . they could say
nothing against it.* I must confess I was shook up and had
trouble finding the right thing to say. I had not really witnessed to Howson Lott, and had considered him a most
unlikely prospect. We don't look for such miracles. I was
sobered that a relative stranger had come to town and won
a man who probably had never been approached in dead
earnest by any Christian in Riverby.

How strange that the conversion of a stubborn old sinner
should be such a sensation in a town full of churches! *Why
marvel ye at this?* Peter asked when the healing of a lame
man created a mighty stir in Jerusalem. Such miracles can
never be commonplace but they should be common. Didn't
our Lord come to set us up in the miracle business?

Far from quelling the opposition, the conversion of Howson Lott seemed to fan the flame. Jeffrey Fullerton seemed
even more vehement. Dr. Price at Main Street Church down-
graded the movement as eccentric and erratic. And, believe
it or not, the fundamentalist preacher at the Bible Church
was cool toward what was going on in Riverby! Could that
have been jealousy? Nothing shows up preachers and
churches more than a real moving of the Spirit. As long as
we play church we are all indistinct in a fog of indefinite gray,
but when it is for real, we are all shown up and are compelled
to declare ourselves. This is uncomfortable for all resters-at-
ease in Zion who wear a PLEASE DO NOT DISTURB sign on
their faces. They resent being put on the spot. Riverby had
been put on the spot and there was a realignment in our
church life. The issue was not Stephen Lynn. He merely
revealed what was already there. He did not put us on the
spot. We were already on the spot, but he made us aware of
it.

Jeffrey Fullerton was wont to dwell on how peaceful church life was in Riverby before "all this uproar" hit town. It was the peace of a graveyard, and now that some of the dead were being raised caretakers of the mortuary were distressed. I remembered that Martha objected to rolling the stone from Lazarus' tomb for fear that it might create an unpleasant situation. It was not too difficult to classify some of the dissent in Riverby.

We were having *not peace but a sword.* Howson Lott had won several of his friends, and was having prayers every morning at his place of business. Some polite pressure was put on the director of the Y and Stephen Lynn was denied further use of the room there. Upon that, Howson Lott set up the large basement room in his home with chairs and a piano and the meetings continued there. Here was one of the erstwhile worst sinners in town leading in a new spiritual movement while prominent churchmen of years standing opposed it!

Sam Bradley, young lawyer, took his stand for Jesus Christ, and began making a deep impression on some of his associates. Helen Page, our soloist, gave up worldly connections and began singing only for her Lord. She had a popular local television program that was dropped when her sponsors would not go along with the new type of program she presented. Lawton Mitchell experienced a great change, cut out his cocktails and dances, removed the bar from his home and stopped serving liquor in the dining room of his department store. He *really* felt the Master's sword, for his wife and family had not been converted to his new position. Lawton Mitchell needs no expositor to explain our Lord's words about divided families because of loyalty to Him. Truly his worst foes were in his own household!

Some of my flock could not stand the heat, and moved to another church where they would not be disturbed by a challenge to serious New Testament discipleship. Some stayed on, very critical of what was happening. Nobody faced a bigger crisis than I myself. So far, I had not actually taken a firm public stand. I thought of those wise words: "The hottest places in hell are reserved for those who in a period of moral crisis maintained neutrality." And there was Edmund Burke's sharp comment: "All that is necessary for the triumph of evil is that good men do nothing." I could not be an innocent bystander, for if I tried being a bystander I would not be innocent. I could not be neither-nor when things were either-or. For me there could *not be peace but a sword.*

3
UNCLE BILL'S CABIN

I decided to spend my vacation in a mountain cabin that belonged to Uncle Bill Blaine. He went along to get me settled down and then returned to Riverby. Uncle Bill is something of a woodsman and a philosopher. Some of his remarks are jewels. He is not too impressed with higher education for everybody. "When everybody is a Ph.D.", he asked, "who'll collect the garbage?"

One Sunday after I had exerted myself more than usual in my preaching, he said, "Reverend, you're pushing the plow."

When I asked him to elucidate, he reminded me that the mule is supposed to pull the plow. "That's what the mule is for." I suppose he meant that I was to roll my burden on the Lord, trust the Holy Spirit to put the sermon over, and not try to do God's part in my preaching. I've mulled that one over a great many times since!

Two weeks with my Bible by a lake in the mountains brought me to a new dedication. I resolved to give more time not just to rest and recreation, or even study, but to reflection and meditation in solitude. I made up my mind not to get so occupied with baggage that I failed to enjoy life's journey. My Lord rose before day to pray in a solitary place. He found both time and place for communion with God—and so must we.

When I returned to Riverby my decision had been made as to the movement Stephen Lynn had begun. Having charge of the program of the next ministers' meeting I asked Lynn to speak. It looked like a frame-up, for a question and answer period developed that ran until one o'clock.

Dr. Price asked Lynn what would happen if all of us preachers abandoned the regular church program for an unorganized movement such as his. Lynn replied that God did not intend that—that he had been called to a special ministry to the whole church and all churches, to gather kindling from all the fellowships to send back to their own churches to rekindle the fire of God there.

At the end of the discussion I arose and stated that I had been blessed by Stephen Lynn's presence in Riverby, and that I considered him to be a chosen servant of the Lord to call us back to New Testament faith and conduct, and that I felt our greatest need to be familiarizing ourselves with the familiar—living what we already know, daring to be just Christians whatever the consequences.

It is one thing to make high resolves in the solitude "far from the madding crowd's ignoble strife," but another to stand by them before a city congregation on Sunday morning. I took the bull by the horns, however, and openly commended the movement Lynn had begun. I decided also to say no more about it after that, for after all *Lynnism* (as some called it) was not the issue, but simply to preach the great truths and call my people to repentance, confession of sin, discipleship, separation from the world, submission to the Lordship of Christ, and the filling of the Holy Spirit. I knew that Stephen Lynn would be leaving soon, but his mantle would not fall on me for every man has his own work and serves his generation by the will of God. He had been used of God to detonate the charge, to crystallize that conviction that had haunted me through the years, and I had resolved to accept the challenge to be "just a Christian," to trust Jesus Christ for everything—and see what happened. I could stay in Riverby indefinitely—*if* I chose the line of least resistance —but I must go to my Lord without the camp bearing His reproach. I could "bring the flag back to the regiment" and adjust the standard to the living of my people—or I could call on the regiment to catch up with the flag. I was sick and tired of hearing a smug lukewarm congregation, rich and increased with goods and needing nothing, sing

> To the old rugged cross I will ever be true,
> Its shame and reproach gladly bear.

God forgive us! It was time to learn that His way means *not peace but a sword.*

Soon after I returned to Riverby, Stephen Lynn made his departure as he had said he would. I began a new chapter in my ministry at Memorial, knowing full well that there are not, and never will be, any perfect churches. I am not a perfectionist (a person who takes great pains and gives them to everybody else). The new Testament churches had essentially the same problems and weaknesses that we have today, but the pastor's temptation is that since we should not expect too much we may settle for too little. I had read A.J. Gordon's dream of how Christ came to his Boston church and how profoundly it changed his life and work. It took him fifteen years to get rid of a paid choir and pew rents in that moss-covered closed corporation before they could grow into a powerful church. It was not a perfect church, but it was a long way nearer that goal than most churches ever travel. After all, the New Testament standard is not imperfection!

I began to call my Laodicea to repentance, to confession of sin and renunciation of the world. Some heard the Saviour at the door, opened their hearts to Him and began to live in fellowship with Him. I was not interested in taking a few of the membership down the street somewhere to start a new church. Why not a new church in the old church? But while that is relatively simple in a young church, it is a complicated procedure in an old establishment covered with as many barnacles as Memorial has. Nor was I remotely interested in an independent church with a nucleus of those who had attended Stephen Lynn's meetings. They began, for the most part, to come to us because I had commended his ministry.

Some of my flock, especially Jeffrey Fullerton, did not welcome them, and feared that we would end up with a nondescript mixture, no longer a denominational church. I had no thought of that. I did not believe in forsaking our great churches because they fall below the standard. We who believe what our churches originally believed were here first. If anybody leaves, let it be those who have departed from the faith and practice with which we started. Why turn the ship over to the mutineers? One old veteran said, "I'm standing where we used to stand, and when my crowd gets right they'll be where I am because I'm where they used to be!"

My dream was to start over with a dedicated Gideon's Band, and seek to infiltrate first the undedicated majority within the church, and beyond that the unreached multitude outside. We must begin the fire with a handful of kindling wood and set the backlog of our unsaved and uncommitted membership on fire next. That would mean, not intensified *church work* but being *just Christians* in shop and office and school and home and wherever one lives and works. After all, every church member should be in what we call "full-time Christian service." It is not reserved for preachers and foreign missionaries!

Of course we would seek a general revival that would transcend all barriers. When such Divine visitations come, all party lines are obscured. When the tide is out, every little shrimp has a puddle of its own, but when the tide comes in all the shrimp are submerged in the great inflow. In wintertime, fences are conspicuous, but at harvest we cannot see the fences because they are hidden in the harvest.

As I said before, all of this sounds good in a cabin by a lake in the mountains, but implementing it in a staid, settled church, rich and increased with goods and needing nothing, is something else altogether. Things began happening both ways. Our Lord said, *He that is not with me is against me: and he that gathereth not with me scattereth.* There are no such people as "inactive church members." They are either gatherers or scatterers, and the right kind of preaching compels men and women to show which side they are on. No longer would my pastorate be the easy-going sinecure it had been in what Jeffrey Fullerton called the good old days at Memorial. There would *not be peace but a sword.*

4
THE DIE IS CAST

I have written earlier about Lawton Mitchell of the department store. He came to see me upon my return. Since he gave up the bar in his home, liquor in his store dining room, and started prayers at his place of business, he had felt the dividing sword. His wife thought he was going off on religion. I went to see her but she was adamant. I told Lawton to read 1 Peter 4:1–5 which explains why some of his former associates think he is strange because he *runs not with them to the same excess of riot* as he used to do.

Helen Page, our soloist, took a class of girls and began a marvelous work with them. Sam Bradley, the young banker, was not in my church but began working with young men in his own church. Lillian Webster gave up her job as a motel hostess because she would not serve liquor in the restaurant. I had preached about Tertullian and how some Christians of his day made images for the pagans. They argued that they were craftsmen and had to make a living. Tertullian answered by asking, "Must you live?" A Christian does not have to live—he has only to be faithful to Jesus Christ.

But I didn't want a church full of mere *Don'ters* who are just as good as trying not to be bad can make them. After all, the Pharisees majored on separation *from*. They wouldn't eat an egg that had been laid on the Sabbath! What we wanted was a radiant positive Christian witness in Riverby, and we were seeing it. The salt was infiltrating the community. It was arousing scorn and opposition on one hand, but on the other it was making its influence felt in lives and homes and places of business. Of course, salt not only heals and purifies, it irritates when rubbed into the sores of humanity. Agonizing decisions and appraisals had to be made. The old days when we coasted along avoiding controversy and confrontation in a pleasant permissiveness were gone. We were no longer fighting sham battles in "a pleasant exercise of give and take" as Joseph Parker used to call it.

My first head-on collision came when Jeffrey Fullerton suggested his nephew, Dr. Winfield Stone, as the speaker for our forthcoming annual Spiritual Emphasis Week. Dr. Stone was a brilliant young liberal professor in our seminary. His views on the inspiration of Scripture, the virgin birth, the deity of Christ and other doctrines were about as far from mine as they could possibly be. I don't think Jeffrey Fullerton knew the difference between truth and error, and he wouldn't care if he did. How can a man sit in church for years and hear the truth—and still not know black from white?

At the deacons' meeting I could have cheerily agreed to Dr. Stone's coming. It would have looked tolerant and broad-minded. To oppose it would appear un-Christlike, selfish, and narrow. But I could not smilingly consent to another teacher in my pulpit, denying all I had tried to preach as though it didn't matter. I thought of 2 John, verses 10 and 11 and plenty more in the New Testament about contending for the faith and sound doctrine. (Dr. Phillips says the early Christians did it in a manner that seems un-Christian to some today.) Then I stated to the deacons that I could not in good conscience consent to Dr. Stone teaching in my pulpit.

Fullerton was enraged. Some stood by me, but others felt it wasn't that critical. Dr. Stone heard about it and let it be known that he would not come. That let me off the hook (in a way) and averted a church showdown, but it pointed up the issue. Word got around and the die was cast. Thereafter it would be *not peace but a sword.*

And rumors were plentiful in Riverby. It was noised abroad that I had gone *way out,* that holy rollers were joining Memorial, that the church faced a split. The confrontation over Dr. Stone made gossip among the brethren, and I was visited by Dr. Wilbur McBane from my seminary. It was part of his assignment up there to pour oil on troubled waters and, like Gamaliel, to keep peace in Jerusalem. In his most diplomatic way, he regretted the friction over Dr. Stone, warned against off-brand movements, and cautioned me against jeopardizing "a brilliant future" by insisting on impossible standards.

"We can only approximate," he assured me, "and achieve a reasonable facsimile of the ideal. Compromises are necessary, for nothing is all white or all black, and we sometimes have to settle for gray."

It was the approach of the church politician. I had known that years ago Wilbur McBane was something of a firebrand himself, but what never could have been done by persecution had been done by promotion. He had been given a top seat in the synagogue, and had not really been heard from since. The prophet had become a priest—and the eagle's wings had been clipped!

I thanked the good doctor, but made no comment. Some weeks later my name was politely removed from one of the boards, but on the other hand, I was invited to speak at our State Assembly. How or why I never knew.

Immediately I faced another test. Should I make the usual pep speech and join the "bland leaders of the bland?" Should I call on "our great denomination" to forget its theological differences, shake the hayseeds out of our hair, and come of age, square our shoulders, regroup our forces and march forward? (What if Joshua had tried that approach after Ai?)

Anyway, that is the pitch if you are smart and on your way up. Then I could say that there is room for all schools of thought among us (but my conscience told me this would be too much room!). Actually, I mused, we are headed in two different directions, and are trying to maintain an image of unity and solidarity that does not exist. The same fountain cannot send forth both bitter water and sweet, and two cannot walk together if they be not agreed. There is a way to preach that sounds bold and straightforward—but really it is the art of *almost* saying something and I did not want to become an expert in that!

So I resolved to tell it like it is—at least to tell it as I saw it—and take the consequences. I felt that we were being honeycombed with false doctrine, infested with worldliness and getting away from the plain people (trying to feed giraffes instead of the sheep). And that's exactly what I decided to tell the State Assembly.

With some my address went over like the proverbial lead balloon; others of like mind responded warmly. Some were afraid to betray any emotion pro or con. I am sure some thought I had clobbered my future with one speech. (I thought of Micaiah when he was called in to prophesy concerning Ahab's venture against Ramoth-gilead. He had a ready-made audience of two kings and four hundred prophets. What an opportunity to make a name for himself and steal the show! I think a modern Billy Sunday would put it this way: "Micaiah's contemporaries must have said, 'Poor Mike! The chance of a lifetime and he blew it!' ")

There are times when a prophet, like Micaiah, sentences himself to a diet of bread and water with one sermon—but if he walks out of the pulpit with a clean conscience and the smile of God, that is his finest hour.

5
CHUCK ROBBINS, MOD
EVANGELIST

It never rains but it pours. When one sets out to follow Christ in dead earnest, one decision follows fast upon another. There is never a dull moment! I had barely recovered from the Doctor Stone episode (and my encounter with Dr. McBane) when a problem of an entirely different sort hit town: Chuck Robbins, colorful, flashy self-styled youth evangelist—complete with sideburns, mod outfit, medallion, and a combo band—held forth for ten days in the city auditorium. A packed house of both teen-agers and oldsters went wild over him. Hundreds of "decisions" were reported. Some of our own young people got into it—and *church* looks pretty tame after that!

Trying the spirits—whether they be of God—can be agonizing business sometimes. In our own church Billy Burns and his kids often had a lively afternoon of games, a supper, and then a season of song, prayer, and testimony. If anybody thinks I favor a dreary austerity among young people he should have attended one of these evening get-togethers. But they ended with a serious and reverent sense of God. Surely no man in his right mind expects teen-agers to act like a Ladies Aid Circle, but the alternative is not an extravaganza scarcely distinguishable from the bedlam of this world except that it is under religious auspices!

Chuck Robbins and his new beat were definitely something cut from different cloth. Billy Burns and his group were not impressed. One does not think of translating Shakespeare into hillbilly vernacular or reducing Beethoven to rock'n-'roll. The idea that we must imitate the world in clothes, language, and music to make the Gospel attractive is not divine but demonic. To begin with, the Gospel was never meant for entertainment. The sin against the Holy Spirit lay in ascribing the work of God to the devil. Is it not equally possible to ascribe the work of the devil to God? I do not believe that spiritually sensitive souls can equate Gospel jazz and hippie hootenannies with the hallelujahs of the redeemed.

It seemed that the best thing to do about the Robbins so-called revival was to overcome evil with good. Instead of pulpit denunciation we would try to offset the extremism with a clear challenge of costly discipleship. Today we adjust the Bible to the individual so that he accepts as inspired only that part of Scripture that speaks to him. Gospel music is being adjusted to the tastes and demands of youth. But God meant that we adjust to the Gospel—not that we fit the Gospel to us. In this epidemic of relevance a preacher can turn his young people off, but he can also cheapen his message for popularity and so develop a superficial band of shallow disciples.

I think of young Jim Elliot who died at the hands of savages on a mission field. Before he left the States he visited a friend one night and watched television. He was convicted later by Psalm 119:37: *Turn away mine eyes from beholding vanity; and quicken thou me in thy way.* And Jim Elliot wrote these words:

I sensed the powerful decentralizing effect on my mind
and affections. It quickens me in ways not of God, defeat-
ing the purpose of prayer to be quickened in ways Divine.
Lord, grant me a disciplined spirit and an obedient body
henceforth!

Producing that kind of young saiņt is slow business. The
road is long but the difference is worth the distance! (And
this was the route we took at Memorial regarding Chuck
Robbins, Mod Evangelist.)

6
RENDERING UNTO CAESAR

Richard Wilkerson, our representative to Washington, showed great interest in the new movement that began in Riverby with Stephen Lynn. Although not a member of Memorial Church, he attended frequently and spoke once to our men's meeting. I never can tell whether a politician's religion is part of his politics or whether his politics is part of his religion, but no man can be a disciple of our Lord long in these times without running headlong into some situation that shows which side he is really on.

Our district, liquor-wise, is wet. A large distillery on the edge of town, and the drinking public generally, made their influence felt in three referendums through the years. The drys always lost but kept on trying, and when the last effort was made Wilkerson was our representative. Would he stand by his professed Christian principles or side with the majority?

When I encountered him a few days before the voting was to take place I made bold to ask him where he stood. He replied that he represented his constituency rather than himself, and although this was a local and not a national issue, he would go with the majority in his district. I reminded him that he claimed to be a Christian, and that his first loyalty was to Jesus Christ, whether in Washington or on any issue.

Of course, to side with Christ instead of the constituency would keep many a man from returning to Washington after the next election! In a tobacco-growing district, for instance, for a congressman to line up with the forces that are aroused over the health hazard and want at least the advertising curtailed, might mean political suicide.

We must, however, do more than take a negative stand *against* something. We are not to be conformed to this world, but we must be more than mere nonconformists. There must be the witness of a transformed life. How far should a man in public office go in practising his Christianity? How long would he last if he put his religion first? What would happen if any leader—from the president down—should dare to name our real trouble—sin—and prescribe the real remedy —Jesus Christ? Is that reserved for churches and taboo in legislative halls just because so many of our people profess other faiths or have no religious faith at all?

At any rate, I went down that line in a sermon one Sunday. Henry Crutchfield, one of our city councilmen, remarked later, "You don't run a city council like a Sunday school." (He must have shelved his Christian convictions, if any, to vote for some of the projects he has approved.) But one councilman, Peter Hobbs, has consistently followed his conscience. He believes that Christians should stand for civic righteousness and try to make conditions better when and where they can. He is not expecting to convert Sodom but believes in bearing a good witness in it. Hobbs feels that he has been saved out of it, is *in* it but not *of* it—that he may go right back into it to let his light shine, for that is the only business Christians have in it. But the going is rough. *In the world ye shall have tribulation* [pressure]. It is *not peace but a sword,* as Riverby Christians were beginning to find out!

Yes, the new social upheaval invaded Riverby as every-where else. To be *in* meant involvement in the race issue, poverty, housing, the youth revolution, and the general worldwide ferment. Clergymen got on the bandwagon, like the four hundred prophets bidding Ahab go up against Ramoth-gilead. Every sensible Christian knows there is a social application of Christianity. The Christian life makes its influence felt in every area. The greatest social reforms have been the by-products of spiritual awakenings like the Wesleyan Revival. Christians render unto Caesar the things that are Caesar's; they are citizens of the commonwealth and should be interested in better living conditions, better educa-tion, better politics, better everything.

The new upheaval, however, would secure the benefits of spiritual revival *without* the revival. There has been no spiritual awakening lately and the process is in reverse. The cart is before the horse. Moreover, the new ferment bears no evidence of being the work of the Spirit of God. If it were, it would not produce the bitterness, the hatred, the violence, the anarchy of these times.

I cannot get excited over the senseless polarization be-tween evangelism and social action. It appears that we are getting more concerned with Lazarus in his poverty than with Dives on his way to hell. Building bigger and better hogpens in the far country has become more important than getting the prodigal back home to the Father. My New Tes-tament does not read that this boy said, "I will arise and apply for government relief".

There is one master program of which all the various issues are scattered pieces. That program is the homogeniza-tion and regimentation of humanity into one faceless mass to be taken over by Antichrist in the last days. Some of these projects are good in themselves—and if they were directed and administered by Spirit-filled Christians would make for better conditions. But the kingdom of heaven cannot be superimposed on an unregenerate society by education, legislation, reformation.

Back of all the confusion in the church lies the fact that so many totally misunderstand God's program. He is not converting civilization, but is taking out a people for His Name. The age will end in cataclysm when Christ returns to set up His kingdom. The world will not be Christianized but should be evangelized.

Well, when I finally got around to preaching this one Sunday morning, it did not enhance my reputation with the avant-garde. Some politicians and professors went out shaking their heads. They agreed that I had gone completely off my rocker. The idea of our Lord returning suddenly and visibly to set things right is always repugnant to kingdom-builders who fear that their long-range plans may be disturbed if we think Jesus may return today. I remember that it was our Lord's announcement of His return when He was on trial that precipitated the violent reaction of the high priest and speeded His execution (Matthew 26:59–67). The priests still rend their garments when His imminent return is emphasized!

7
BRUCE AND HELEN

Bruce Lockerbie had that extra ingredient. Everyone in Riverby who heard him sing as a lad in Sunday school recognized that he had what makes the difference. There was that indefinable quality that always put him over. All agreed that he would go a long way.

Through college and conservatory days he returned often to Riverby and sang for us at Memorial. He and Helen Page had been high-school sweethearts. The affection grew. It would be easy for any man to fall in love with Helen Page! Their duets thrilled us. It was difficult to distinguish between what part of it was human appeal and how much was spiritual, but we forgot all that and just enjoyed them.

Bruce started a television program that became an instant success. Helen shared some of it—at first. Soon it became evident, though, that Bruce, like so many stars who had grown up in a religious background (some had even thought of becoming preachers), was veering toward popular music. Popularity, money, big automobiles—we could see the change. Bruce still had character, but the discerning could detect the departing glow.

Helen began to see that it would mean a major decision, next only to becoming a Christian and her fresh commitment during the days of Stephen Lynn's ministry. Her dedication then had been summed up in the lines,

> Take my voice and let me sing
> *Only, always* for my King.

None of us knew, of course, how many hours Bruce and Helen discussed and debated the matter.

"Can't we be dedicated Christians and still sing popular music? Do we have to be just Gospel singers? Some opera stars are known as real Christians. Don't we need Christians in these areas?"

It was akin to the old hassle over whether one could glorify God in the movies. Some even went so far as to say that a converted night club singer could stay on in the night club (ending her program, I presume, by singing "I'd rather have Jesus!").

After all, Bruce was only singing pop music. Maybe that would have been easier in the old "Moonlight and Roses" days when the emphasis was on romance instead of sex. But for Helen it meant singing *only, always,* for the King or singing for the world. She could not do both. The Master's sword had separated her from working both sides of the street.

All we know is that one night in one of our great church assemblies—Helen Page was in demand far and wide—she was to sing the solo. Now our assemblies were not fussy about using only full-time Gospel singers. Jane Hathaway, fresh from Hollywood, had gone over big the night before. (Almost anything goes with our church folk these days.)

But that night I sensed what many did not know. When Helen stood to sing, something told me that she had been

through the refining fire. It was written on her face. She had
a great chance to sway a big audience with sheer artistry but
instead she simply sang:

> Jesus, I my cross have taken,
> All to leave and follow Thee;
> Destitute, despised, forsaken,
> Thou, from hence, my all shalt be.

The congregation was aware of another Presence that
night. It was not "that special something" but "that Special
Someone" who made the difference. There was a lovely face,
a matchless voice and exquisite rendition, but flesh was not
glorying in God's Presence. Helen Page was singing her way
out of the greatest test of her life. I thought of Jenny Lind
and how she reached her greatest heights after her heart was
broken. We were not hearing art but heart.

Helen Page would sing henceforth: *only, always,* for her
King.

8
"LORD, DON'T LET HIM CATCH ON."

Howson Lott couldn't understand it.

He was a hardened sinner before his wonderful conversion. Through the prayers of his wife and the ministry of Stephen Lynn, he came to a glorious experience. I have never seen a better illustration of 2 Corinthians 5:17: *Therefore if any man be in Christ, he is a new creature: old things are passed away; behold, all things are become new.*

Howson Lott was a transformed man. Whatever he did, he always meant business. He was practical, forthright, straightforward. He came to church for every event he could possibly attend. He had lost so much time, he said, that now he wanted to make up for as much as he could. He knew little theology, but I have always said that the happiest man in the world is a young Christian before he has met too many Bible scholars! Every time I saw him in his corner at church I felt like praying, "Lord, don't let him catch on. Don't let him notice how many deacons are absent. He thinks he is supposed to be here and doesn't know any better. Keep him in this blessed ignorance!"

To Howson Lott, being a Christian was a brand-new amazing experience. It was a rebuke to my ministerial complacency. One thing he could not understand. He wondered why most church folk were so apathetic about what was to him so wonderful. It seemed to him that people who had been Christians much longer than he should be still happier and more excited since they had had more time to explore what to him was new country.

I tried to reason that most Christians had made a profession of faith maybe as children before the contrast between what they had been and what they had become was so vivid. Then of course I knew that many more had never been converted at all so they knew nothing of Howson Lott's ecstasy. And even true Christians tend to get over it and leave their first love. But such explanations never did satisfy me and I dared not suggest to Howson Lott that we tend to cool off. He would find that out soon enough by observation if not by experience. I knew the familiar analogy of how fervent courtship gradually settles to the routine of day-by-day married life and the earlier manifestations of love give way to a calmer and deeper affection. But that never had appealed to me as a good explanation of Christians who change from boiling to lukewarm. After all, my Lord called on lukewarm Laodicea to come to a boil!

The problem of how to channel new converts into the regular life of the church without extinguishing their flame has bothered me from the start. Somehow in the process we smother what we need most to preserve. But first love need not depart nor the flame burn low. Gipsy Smith, when asked how he kept fresh in soul well into the eighties, replied, "I have never lost the wonder." Thank God for some precious souls who have kept the fire going and growing and glowing. Howson Lott is one of them. He has made more progress after a late start than some of my flock after forty years. It is disturbing that he has more zeal and zest than Jeffrey Fullerton who has been a deacon most of his life. It may be a little irritating to some who don't believe in getting excited about being saved and on the way to heaven.

Next to not being a Christian at all, what greater tragedy can there be than getting used to being a Christian? Howson Lott can't understand that. It bothers me, too.

9
WISDOM FROM BROTHER DAN

I was troubled by conditions in my own denomination. The authority of the Scriptures was being denied. Error was being taught. Worldliness infested and infected the churches. A social gospel was trying to change society without changing hearts. We were getting away from the common people. Anarchy in the world, apostasy in the professing church, apathy in the true church—this infernal triumvirate was everywhere in evidence.

What should I do? Some were for leaving the Establishment to start an independent church. I respected the convictions of those who felt this was the only way to come out of Babylon, to go to our Lord without the camp bearing his reproach—but I could not see this course for myself.

Others would turn politician and go along with the trend. Some would play it safe trying to project an image of unity and solidarity that did not exist. These evils will not go away if we merely refuse to look at them.

Some said, "Don't rock the boat!" but I decided to join those who preferred rocking the boat to wrecking the boat. In such a time silence is consent—not golden—but yellow! The shepherd sees the wolf coming. That is the right time to see the wolf—not after he is among the flock! We are sheep among wolves, and must look out for wolves among the sheep.

There was a rising tide of feeling among preachers and laity in the churches. A mass meeting was called for. By a majority—but not unanimous—vote, Memorial Church extended a welcome. Headquarters heard about it and Dr. McBane called to remonstrate, but we went ahead.

It was a terrific evening. The church was filled. A host of preachers—not many "prominent" pastors but plenty of fine earnest men—was present. Of course we would be called calamity howlers, witch hunters, viewers-with-alarm, disturbers of the peace. At least we were not crying *Peace!* when there was no peace. There were fireworks aplenty, denunciation of false teachers, even suggestions of a coming break with the Establishment. There was, of course, a rabble rouser or two with more heat than light.

We were right theologically. We were right in calling attention to the perils of the hour. We were right in forthright protest, but somehow I had a feeling that all this was not enough. It would take more than pulpit rebuke and the belligerent affirmation of our othodoxy—some do not know the difference between being belligerent and being militant! All of this had been done before only to degenerate into personality conflicts, bitter squabbles, too many prima donnas on the stage, too many chiefs and not enough Indians.

The evening wore on and we almost had an anticlimax when one dear brother took thirty minutes to say what could have been said in ten. As Uncle Bill Blaine put it, "The harder he tried, the worse he couldn't!"

If the meeting had ended there, we would have been compelled to call it "too much wind and not much rain." Dan Goforth saved the day. We all knew and loved Brother Dan.

He was never *Doctor* or even *Reverend,* always Brother Dan. He had given most of his life to one little town, but he was the bishop of that bailiwick. Given to meditation and prayer, he had never joined the ministerial rat race. Hours with his Bible had given him what degrees and travel and cleverness and politics had never bestowed on the rest of us. I had observed that, for all our bigger churches and clerical prestige, we were compelled to give deference to a wisdom and saintliness in him which we had not attained. There are diverse ways of gaining the world and losing one's soul. Brother Dan had little of this world but he had kept his soul in good repair!

Brother Dan began by saying that we had not really come to the root of the matter. "Ephesus was sound in doctrine and contended earnestly for the faith, but had left her first love. Mere fundamentalism is not enough. We have as many things to repent of as the liberals," he declared. "Not the same things but as many things. Sins of omission, commission, disposition—these are as grievous in God's sight as theological error. Our Lord's last word to the church was *Repent.* Only a visitation of God can meet our need today. While revival is God coming down, repentance is the under side of revival. This is our part: God's people humbling themselves, praying, seeking God's face and turning from their wicked ways."

Brother Dan said he saw very few signs of revival because we will not repent. "There is no use trying to do the second and third thing until we do the first thing."

When Brother Dan sat down, the moderator of the meeting made some rather awkward remarks and we adjourned. Some thought we ran out of steam and that the program fizzled out at the close. I came out convinced that the real problem had been stated by Brother Dan, but as usual we accepted it as information and were dismissed. We will do anything and everything else in our churches today but repent. Yet a fresh confrontation with God and an outpouring of His Spirit would dispel error and worldliness, meet social issues and produce real unity as no amount of effort in the flesh could ever do. These evils that beset us would fade in the light of God's holiness. The cheap and tawdry tricks we borrow from the world to promote the Gospel would vanish as we hang our heads in shame that we had ever used them.

But what Sunday morning congregation is in a mood to repent? Laodicea is rich, increased with goods, and has need of nothing. Our Lord bade the original Laodicea repent, but that church never repented and so was spewed out of His mouth. Lukewarm institutional Christianity today will not be zealous, will not come to a boil, so it faces the same judgment. But our Lord extended a second proposition to anyone who would hear His voice, open the door and live in fellowship with Him. He is gathering out His *Anyones* today and I had been seeing that process going on in Memorial Church and all over Riverby.

Yes, I decided, my duty was still to call the church to repent, but also to call out the church within the church— that Master's Minority of the listening ear, the open door, and the table of fellowship. Meanwhile we pray for a visitation of God in revival. It must be revival—our Lord's return or ruin. At present God is moving in a thousand ways among true Christians of all churches. That is the true ecumenical movement. It cannot be organized for that would kill it. So I had to work in two dimensions, calling the professing church to repentance and working with the true church, the dedicated minority, to reach the undedicated majority and the unsaved multitudes outside.

One thinks of Malachi and how most of his congregation met his calls to repentance with a tired *Wherein?* Yet there was a minority whose hearts were filled with the fear of God, whose minds were fed on thoughts of God, whose tongues were busy with the things of God, and whose names were written in the book of God. The true preacher will meet a barrage of *Whereins* today, but he will delight in the fellowship of the Remnant who await the day when the Lord comes to make up his jewels.

I would try to reach this Remnant!

10
LAWTON MITCHELL UNDERSTOOD

If any man in Riverby knew the meaning of *not peace but a sword,* it was Lawton Mitchell. Since his conversion, some changes in his department store (like stopping the sale of liquor in the dining room) cost him customers and financial loss. Some of his business associates viewed him with curiosity, to say the least. Club members marvelled that ginger ale had taken the place of cocktails, and shady jokes were no longer told by him or laughed at either. But the sword flashed most at home. Lawton, Junior, couldn't dig the new image his father had created. Barbara, his teen-age daughter, had problems arising from her dad's introduction of a new way of living into the big house on Sunset Drive.

The supreme test was provided by Julia, his wife. I made no headway when I talked it over with her.

"Where does this put me?", she asked, "and what about my side of this story? Am I supposed to rearrange my habits, adjust my social life, to square with this religious brainstorm that has hit him and others in Riverby? Remember, this is *his* conversion, not mine. I thought religion was supposed to unite homes, not split them. Think of the embarrassing explanations I'm having to make these days. He has a right to his own convictions, but he is a man with a family and his convictions cannot determine the conduct of the rest of the family. What is going to happen if we keep this up—the head of the house going in one direction, and the rest taking another road? Lawton is a good man, and he hasn't tried to legislate for us, but there is this conflict and it will pull us in two both individually and as a family."

I was aware from the start that it was practically a waste of time trying to help Julia Mitchell see this. The natural man cannot receive the things of the Spirit, and she would never understand until she was converted. One might as well try to describe a sunset to a blind man or talk nuclear physics to a monument in a city park. Julia Mitchell was an educated woman, but a Ph.D. gives no advantage in these matters. I thought of the old saying, "Nothing is settled until it is settled right—and nothing is settled right until it is settled with God." Until this was settled with God it just wouldn't be settled. There might be an effort to patch it up by agreeing to disagree.

Lawton and I prayed and talked it over by the hour. He realized that for his family there could be no conformity without conversion. I had no ready answers and easy solutions.

"Your family may be converted and for that we shall pray and work," I told him, "but loyalty to Christ does not always have a storybook ending where everybody lives happily forever after. For the rest of your days it may be *not peace, but a sword.*"

Lawton Mitchell understood. Before his conversion he had been a hardheaded, practical business man. Now his sanctified good sense and calm judgment stood him in good stead. He was under no illusions. He had counted the cost. On that day when he took up his cross to follow the Master, he was aware that this would be no religious lark. He was headed for a pilgrimage, not a picnic; a fight, not a frolic. He had signed up for the duration. Stephen Lynn had made it clear, and I had tried to follow up the initial instructions: this would be no glorified excursion. Lawton Mitchell had geared himself under God for reality. He demanded no happy ending. Like the Hebrew children before the fiery furnace, he had resolved, "God is able to deliver me but if not, I will be faithful anyway." Would that some weak-kneed members of my flock with far fewer problems had his fortitude!

11
NO TURNING BACK

I was actually pastor of two churches in one. There was the fellowship that had grown out of the Stephen Lynn movement—*Lynnites,* we were dubbed in some quarters. Howson Lott, Lawton Mitchell, Helen Page, Sam Bradley, and many others—a Gideon's Band who had chosen the road of total commitment and full-time discipleship *(not peace but a sword).* There was also the regular membership untouched by the challenge to take Christ seriously—the average run-of-the-mill church folks, Sunday-morning Christians, and others who showed up at Christmas and Easter ("the holly and lilies crowd," Uncle Bill Blaine called them).

Here were two churches meeting under the same roof—as far apart as East from West—and never the twain would meet. Should we keep up the farce of trying to be one church going two directions? There are worse things than division. Our Lord was the greatest divider of all time, and plainly declared in His *not peace but a sword* pronouncement that He came to divide even families. Would it not be plain honesty for Memorial Church to become two churches rather than present an image of unity that did not exist? I longed to be shepherd of a flock, not the keeper of a menagerie!

Before I came to Riverby there had been some agitation to sell the downtown church building and build a new edifice out in suburbia. This gained momentum after the new spiritual movement began. The majority of the membership (the socially prominent, and all who had no interest whatever in the new emphasis on taking Christ seriously) wanted to start a new church where they could rest at ease in Zion untroubled by a call to self-denying, cross-bearing discipleship. The rest of us wanted to stay on in the old building and make it a people's church downtown. The devil and sin were still downtown, and we felt that the light is needed most where the darkness is most intense.

But what about all the financial and legal ramifications as to ownership of the present building? We had read of disgraceful court fights over churches, and were determined not to lose our testimony in a battle of lawyers. Above all, there was First Corinthians, chapter six, about going to law before the unjust and not before the saints. If we could not settle our own problems within the church, what business did we have telling the world that Christ is the Answer to every problem? We are exhorted by Paul to endure wrong and suffer ourselves to be defrauded.

The day came when two sheets of paper were laid on the table before the pulpit. All who wanted to move to suburbia were asked to sign on one, and the rest of us on the other. Terms were finally agreed upon for the building to be retained by those who chose to remain. The day came when a reduced congregation gathered to rededicate an old building refurbished to begin a second chapter in the life of Memorial Church. We were the butt of some wry humor and cynical jokes and unfavorable publicity. The suburban congregation would call as pastor Dr. Stone who had been the first storm center of a series when I opposed his coming to speak at Spiritual Emphasis Week.

If I had imagined that a new era of sweetness and light would dawn after all this transition, I would have been cured of that notion in short order. The minute a Christian or a church takes the stand we took, they become the target of the powers of darkness in a hundred subtle forms. There would be times when in dejection I would almost long for the carefree days before I ever set out on this course of *not peace but a sword*. Had I attempted too much too soon?

But I always came out of the Slough of Despond singing with Billy Burns and his kids:

> The cross before me, the world behind me,
> No turning back, no turning back.
> I have decided to follow Jesus,
> No turning back, no turning back.

12
PENTECOST WAS ITS OWN PUBLICITY

My heart was hungry for revival. I had read of the mighty movings of God in the past, the Wesleyan and early American Awakenings, the Welsh Revival, the Shantung Revival in China. I was weary of human efforts to produce and promote revival, including my own. The new techniques sounded too much like David's new cart for the ark, Rehoboam's shields of brass to replace the golden shields that Shishak had stolen.

One of the promoters of the Chuck Robbins hippie extravaganza of some months past had all the answers. "You can't do it with prayer meetings and the old campmeeting methods," he affirmed. "We're living *now,* not *then.* You have to blow it up with the mass media. The kids will come if you bring in some Gospel rock and combo. You'll die of old age sitting around waiting for the fire to fall."

I spent an afternoon with old Mr. Davies. Too feeble to get to church, this antiquated Welshman was a lad in the great Revival early in the century. He still had vivid memories of it, and the smell of the fire was still on him. I mentioned publicity.

"Pentecost was its own publicity," he replied. "Peter and John didn't hand out placards all over Jerusalem. First, it happened—and then came the publicity. We are advertising it before it happens—and it doesn't happen. First, let's have it, and then let the press write it up as they will."

But *how?* I called the faithful to prayer and for weeks we waited on God in repentance and confession of sin. I was astounded at how much evil came to light among the best of my people, and how much needed to be straightened out. It was so in my own heart. Eventually there came to us a spirit of expectancy. We scanned the skies, as it were, for a cloud the size of a man's hand. We waited in eagerness to see in what mysterious way God would work "His wonders to perform."

At length, in fear and trembling, I announced a week of special services. Nothing happened the first night. Next night a newcomer to the meetings came forward. He was Red McGuire, a barber, an alcoholic whose family was about to break up. He had tried everything but Jesus Christ and was desperate. In the prayer room a little past midnight he was converted. He neither wept nor shouted, but the Red McGuire who rose from his knees that night was not the same wretch who came to church at seven thirty. Next night he brought his wife and two children and a couple of old buddies. Every one of them went to the prayer room. His wife was a Christian already, but a beaten and discouraged poor soul, and no wonder after years of living with what looked like a hopeless drunk. She came into a glorious fresh experience and the others professed faith in Christ.

By the end of the week, Red had a pew full of old friends he had brought by one means or another. They were a miscellaneous aggregation and not exactly from the elite side of town—but there they were. Red had not read any books on how to do it. If he had, he probably wouldn't have done it!

All he knew was that he had found a new life, and it was too good to keep. He knew scores of jaded souls who needed what he had found, and he simply brought them along to where he thought they could find it. On the last night of the week I pointed out that we had before us an illustration of what everybody believed theoretically, but few ever practiced. We had all known that by simple arithmetic, if everybody present at church brought somebody else next night, by week's end the church wouldn't hold them. Red wasn't trying out any theory—this was simply the spontaneous overflow of a man who had drunk deeply of new life, and this pewful of "prospects" was the outflow and overflow of the inflow of that new life.

Then I surprised even myself by announcing (without consulting anybody) another week of special services.

Red McGuire was not the only one who brought friends to the meetings. Lawton Mitchell brought most of his office force, and Howson Lott showed up night after night with some of his business associates and civic club members. Helen Page brought several of her music class, and Sam Bradley inveigled two or three from his bank to look in on what was going on. I had wondered what I would preach about, but the usual sermons were not necessary. We sang; each night someone gave a fresh, glowing testimony. There was a short Bible message because I was not converted to the theory that we should not preach and quote Scripture to possible converts—just tell our experience. There was a group in town pushing that angle but *faith cometh by hearing, and hearing by the word of God.*

The meetings each night did not follow the usual pattern. People were converted; new Christians witnessed to the new life they had found in Christ. Red McGuire had never spoken in public before, and his testimony lacked much in grammar—but it melted hearts. At the other end of the spectrum Lawton Mitchell and Helen Page spoke with more finesse, but with no less reality.

What thrilled me was that nothing was "worked up." I was not pushing and promoting and striving each night to see if we could drum up a bigger crowd next night. No prizes were offered to whoever brought the most prospects next night. No new Bibles were promised to the oldest grandmother present next evening. (I had not read in my New Testament that after Pentecost Peter and John said, "Let's shoot for five thousand next time!" Nor had John the Baptist offered a free camel to whoever brought most baptismal candidates to the Jordan.) All this was spontaneous, unrehearsed, voluntary. No flamboyant ads were run in the papers. A new Christian is the best advertisement Christianity ever put out, and the word was getting around in Riverby. There was plenty of talk—both pro and con—about strange goings-on at Memorial Church.

It was on Monday night of the second week that Phil Thomas came down the aisle. Phil was president of the senior class in his high school, son of the editor of the *Riverby Record,* and leading player on the football team. He had a future in athletics, and the scouts had discovered him, but Billy Burns, our own youth director, and some fellows from a nationwide youth organization had borne their witness. Phil came to say that he had chosen to forget an athletic career for Christian service. The effect was electric, and it permeated the high school.

Then came the blow that stunned everybody. On Wednesday Phil was killed on the highway in a head-on collision with a drunken driver. The funeral was on Friday. I went to a packed church numb, and fearfully wondering, "What will the kids think? How will they interpret this? Will they ask, 'How do you put this together? After all, God didn't want Phil for a missionary.' "

But God came to my help. I simply said, "This life is only an apprenticeship for the next and *his servants shall serve him* [there] (Revelation 22:3). The next life is not an eternal vacation. We get ready here. Phil Thomas did the first thing: he made a total decision once and for all. He did not have time to work it out here, but he enlisted not for time but for eternity, and he will take up there under better conditions what he started here."

Then we broke all rules for funerals and stood to sing "Take Time To Be Holy" with emphasis on the closing verse:

Take time to be holy,
Be calm in thy soul;
Each thought and each motive
Beneath His control;
Thus led by His Spirit
To fountains of love,
THOU SOON SHALT BE FITTED
FOR SERVICE ABOVE.

I extended an invitation and sixty-seven young people came forward as if to say, "We'll take Phil's place."

Next day the Riverby *Daily News* had a story, MEMORIAL PASTOR TURNS FUNERAL INTO REVIVAL. Mr. Davies was right. Pentecost was its own publicity. Have the revival and the write-up will follow!

The revival went into the third week and still Memorial Church overflowed. Preachers from other churches slipped in to observe. I remembered how in the Welsh Revival outstanding preachers came, but they did not preach; they sat in the congregation like everybody else. They did not need big preachers—they had God!

One of our visitors was Baxter Rogers, pastor of a most liberal church uptown. He had preached the truth in earlier years, but not lately. He came for three nights, and on the following Sunday he stood in his own pulpit and announced his return to the old paths. Several influences had brought all this about, but the revival detonated the charge, brought things to a head. His sermon that Sunday was like an earthquake in that Ichabod Memorial, and the walls of that mausoleum reverberated. The new Baxter Rogers was not received with open arms—he immediately joined the society of *Not Peace But A Sword!*

The devil does not take such visitations of God lying down. We were well aware that we were up against *the unseen power that controls this dark world, and spiritual agents from the very headquarters of evil* (Ephesians 6:12, in J.B. Phillips' *The New Testament in Modern English*). Opposition ranged from bitter censure to cynicism and clever sarcasm. The newspapers were not shouting *hallelujahs.* From some pulpits came unexpected criticism. We were treated to the strange spectacle of scribes and Pharisees deriding the revival while publicans and sinners flocked to it! A strange alignment of the citizens of Riverby became evident. We expected antagonism from entrenched evil, but found some strange bedfellows in the camp of our adversaries.

At the end of the third week I was exhausted. I slipped

away for an evening with Mr. Davies. The old Welshman had kept abreast of the meetings. He advised me to close the services. "You can overdo a good thing," was his judgment, "and turn victory into defeat. Satan takes advantage of weariness, and introduces evils born of exhaustion. The human constitution can stand only so much. You cannot go on forever holding meetings that end late in the night."

Then he advanced a philosophy of revivals: "After all, revivals are not supposed to last. They bring a subnormal church back to normal, and if they continued indefinitely things might become abnormal! Indeed, revivals should not be necessary—and would not be—if we grew as we should in grace and the knowledge of Christ. Springtime doesn't last; courtship doesn't last; they serve a purpose, and we go on from there. A revival is like a sale in a department store. It is more spectacular, but the main business is done in the daily, year-round merchandising. So it is with the church."

I incorporated that wise counsel in my sermon next Sunday, and announced the end of the special services.

Some were disappointed and wanted the meetings to go on. They were good souls who wanted to live in a revival all the time, and reminded me of what a Methodist bishop once said about a certain sect who would get to heaven, he thought, if they didn't run past it! These dear people had neglected their homes going to meetings for three weeks. It provided diversion from humdrum living, but nobody can live on the mountain top forever. It was time to bring the vision down from the clouds to the cobblestones, and apply the mystery to the misery, rub the salt into the decaying world around us.

13
VIVAL AND REVIVAL

What a blessing had come to Riverby! Over a hundred new converts had united with Memorial Church. Many had joined elsewhere. Hundreds of Christians had come to a new experience. Some ministers had begun a new chapter in their own lives. Attention had been focused on Jesus Christ for three weeks, and the press had recognized in one way or another that God was in town. There had been criticism, but whether individuals were sad, mad, or glad, anything was better than nothing! Some had come to Memorial Church and had received a charge, while others had been shocked— but all paid tribute to Divine electricity.

This was a better way to meet issues than by condemning them. The best answer to the *demon-stration* of the powers of darkness is a *demonstration* of the power of God. What better way to deal with liberalism than by proving what God's Word can do today when presented in the power of the Spirit? One liberal preacher had been awakened and won back to the fold. Anybody can condemn false doctrine—and there is indeed a place for that—but is it not better to overcome evil with good? We lament worldliness, but the revival had led hundreds to renounce the world through the expulsive power of a new affection. We had been arguing evangelism versus social action, but

Spirit-filled Christians were now making their impact in all areas of life.

Strange as it may seem, however, revivals do not always bring an unmixed blessing. They solve many problems, but sometimes create new ones. Revival is not the answer to everything. Pentecost did not convert Jerusalem. The city went on to judgment. Results depend on how different people react to revival. When our meetings closed, some resolved to continue somewhere else. They gathered in homes and a local church or two took advantage of the ferment to begin revivals of their own. That would have been wonderful, but strange and weird experiences were sought and wildfire broke out. A few of my own people were carried away with this. Of course I was blamed for it and, back of me, Stephen Lynn, for starting a form of religious "hysteria" in Riverby. Although I clarified my position in several sermons, false reports seemed to outrun the truth.

Wherever there is a true work of God, I discovered that Satan employs not only opposition but *imitation* to defeat it. Instead of uprooting the wheat he sows tares. I was much depressed when a wildfire evangelist, hearing of the revival, moved into another part of town with a big tent and began holding meetings that had never been experienced in our city before. The tent was more like a circus carousel than a place of worship. The disturbance became so great that neighborhood residents protested.

Again I consulted my oracle, dear Brother Davies. His words were typical.

"Satan is the Mock Angel. Wherever Moses performs a miracle, look out for Jannes and Jambres! Such extremism always shows up in revivals. It was true in Wales. When God manifests Himself, Satan shows up with a counterfeit. The false implies the true."

But some people have great difficulty seeing this. They imagine that everything should roll along in apple-pie order with no confusing complications. They do not understand the kind of world we are in—or the nature of our adversary. They are like the dog that was always getting licked in fights with every cur he met. His owner said, "He's a good fighter, but a poor judge of dogs." We must not underestimate our adversary. Neither must we underestimate our Ally.

"If God be for us, who can be against us?" On this I was resolved to rely.

When the special meetings ended and I began to stress *patient continuance in well doing,* I soon discovered that this would separate the men from the boys, as we say, and sift out the undependables. Some who started with a bang soon ended in a bog. They ran around to every special meeting, but knew nothing of loyalty to a local church in season and out. They were like the man who wanted to sing in a certain church choir, but did not wish to belong to that church. He said that he was a member of the invisible church whereupon the pastor advised him to go join an invisible choir. Too many members of the invisible church are invisible at church on Sunday!

It sounded like I was devaluing the importance of special meetings when I declared that the main ministry of the church is not in revivals or evangelistic campaigns, but in the daily witness of Spirit-filled Christians. This does not make headlines and is not spectacular. Newspapers do not write up faithful saints living for God in homes and shops and offices and schools in the humdrum daily grind. These unusual revivals and crusades have their place, but to live only for them is like making everything of Thanksgiving Day, but living ungratefully the rest of the year.

So the real test began at Memorial Church. We could not live on the momentum of a past revival. There must be fresh manna and fresh oil for each day. I remembered that after Pentecost the Jerusalem church became an exclusive closed corporation, and it took persecution to scatter the Christians everywhere in effective witnessing. There were three thousand additions at Pentecost, but thereafter the Lord added daily (Acts 2:41, 47). We had experienced a mass influx. Could we now see the Lord add daily as He did long ago?

Some of the froth subsided when the more excitable element joined other groups in town. There remained a fine residue of Christians who had both ability and dependability. They continued to bring their friends on Sunday and on Wednesday night, and there were conversions and additions week after week. The publicity given us during the revival had centered some attention on us, and the curious dropped in. But we cannot have revivals all the time and the problem was survival. How can the church survive the pressures of today and not only survive but grow and go and glow?

I was convinced that the answer to survival is not occasional revival but *vival*. There is no such word, but Uncle Bill Blaine had said, "If we had more 'vival', we wouldn't need revivals." He meant that if we had more day-by-day normal Christianity we wouldn't need special spells of rejuvenating the church. (Christians grow like boys grow—by food, rest, and exercise—and it would be foolish to starve most of the time, then have certain periods when we majored on eating, resting, and exercising.) But, to use my simile again, it is more exciting to go on a splurge and celebrate Thanksgiving in a big way than to live thankfully all the year. And that does not rule out Thanksgiving Day either!

I announced that, following our Revival, *vival* would now

begin! I also stated in the Sunday sermon that if we had enough *vival, re*vivals would not be necessary. Some of my listeners looked a little confused, and others were jolted, but maybe we need to be jolted into a new appraisal of the whole subject. I am sure some of my critics shook their heads in despair when the *Daily News* garbled things (as they do so often), and reported that I had announced, VIVAL TO FOLLOW REVIVAL TO INSURE SURVIVAL!

14

RED MCGUIRE

When Red McGuire called me to the hospital to pray for him there was little hope for his recovery. The doctor saw only a terminal case. But ever since Red was converted he had been reading his Bible. He had read James 5 and he took it at face value. He had faith to be healed. He asked me to bring some of *the elders of the church* and a bottle of oil, for he wanted it done according to the scriptural procedure.

I had trouble finding elders who had faith for more than the usual prayers for the sick—the kind offered in most churches on prayer-meeting nights. (Such prayers always struck me as being rather tame and so restricted by *ifs* that the sick gathered from them but scant encouragement to expect a miracle.) It would have to be a miracle in Red's case, but he believed God would heal him. He had read no books on healing, nor did he have any theories on the subject. It was not sheer desperation—he simply believed God would heal him. I learned more from him on that visit than he learned from me.

At length I arrived at his bedside with such elders as I could muster. The average run-of-the-mill Christian today believes that God *can* do miracles, but few think He *will* in any given case. We gathered around Red; I anointed him with oil as he had requested, and we prayed. A week later he was at home and on the way to complete recovery. His doctor was a Christian, and could say only that a Power greater than ourselves had evidently intervened.

I advised Red not to publicize it unduly, but I might as well have told a radio station not to broadcast. He published it everywhere with all the colorful emphasis of which he was peculiarly capable. This was not just the usual, and when word got around I was besieged with calls from others in a plight such as Red's had been. I answered some with varied results. Some were healed, some died. This was a mystery to some but the initiated understood. Mother Walker, one of our oldest members, understood. Forty years ago the doctors had practically given her up. The doctors are dead now, but she isn't! She knows that some blessings are for "those choice spirits so simple and stedfast in faith, and so completely detached from the world as to be able sincerely and un-reservedly to place themselves in God's hands" as stated by J. Plessis in the *Life of Andrew Murray*.

Of course I soon gained a reputation as having gone into the healing business. There is an old proverb, "Whoever marries a mountain woman marries the mountain." Let one be involved in just one case of miraculous healing and all the faith-healers claim him. No matter how I explained it from the pulpit, I had joined their ranks in the public eye. Some of the best known and most respected of the great preachers had gone much farther than I, but it made no difference. There are many off-brand and way-out movements majoring on almost every doctrine of the faith, the work of the Spirit, the Lord's return, healing—you name it. It is Satan's clever device to scare us away from the true understanding and appropriation of all these truths. We're so scared we'll get out on a limb that we never get up the tree!

Far greater saints than I will ever be have never settled all the mysteries on this subject. But I have observed that while scholars and theologians sometimes are unable to get low enough and childlike enough to enter into its blessings, some poor troubled soul—like the sick woman who pressed through the crowd to reach Jesus—may touch Him while others only throng Him. And those who touch Him are made perfectly whole.

15
BEN COLE

Billy Burns left us to take graduate studies. That left us without a youth leader at Memorial Church. Following the death of Phil Thomas and the revival, our young people had developed a core of deeply dedicated youth with a seriousness far above the average. They had seen God at work and had a sense of His holiness. They had seen the difference between the radiant reverent joy of the Lord and the cheap hilarity that had grown out of the hippie crusade of months past, plaguing Riverby still with its pitiful parody.

But still we were polarized in Riverby by these two concepts. The only other alternative was the dull, dry church youth programs without any excitement true or false. How anybody could expect teen-agers to find any satisfaction in a dreary hour of lifeless singng and reading from quarterlies was beyond me.

We wondered who would take Billy Burns' place, but God always has the next man in the wings. Ben Cole came to us from college and seminary. Much that he had heard at both places did not take. He did his own studying and praying and thinking and came out with some convictions of his own not shared by the new school. If some oldster had advanced them they might have been credited to senility, and written off as the gripings of diehard reactionaries. But Ben Cole was young and looked like anything but the blue-nosed type so often lampooned in cartoons.

He had attended our revival and had also looked in on the Chuck Robbins crusade. He was ready to take on all comers and squared off first on a television panel with Chuck Robbins himself who was in town for a one-night return engagement.

Chuck led off by saying that he was not opposed to the old hymns and Gospel songs. "I was brought up on them," he said, "and they have their place in Sunday formal church services. But we are in a new day with a problem generation of youth and the old style approach will not work. We must relate to youth with music that appeals to them. We must speak their language and it even helps to wear their kind of clothes. Relevance is the word, and if we are not in their groove we are wasting our time. I believe the end justifies any means we can use."

Ben Cole replied, "For one thing, I would enjoy a moratorium on that word "relevance." The pitch today is, gear everything to youth. To hear some people talk, you'd think young people had just been invented! The teen-ager is at the center of everything and everything must be revamped to please him. In home, school, and church, we adjust to youth instead of asking youth to adjust to time-honored scriptural standards that were here long before this generation came along.

"We are trying to make Christ acceptable to youth when the big issue with youth—as with everybody else—is, how am I made acceptable to Christ? I hear it said that the great doctrines of the Christian faith mean nothing to people today, so we must devise a new theology or at least a new phraseology. But why not teach the great truths and help

people to understand them? Youth can be taught to appreciate great literature, great art, and great music without reducing them to the jargon of this age. I believe they can be taught
the great Bible doctrines and learn to appreciate the great
saints of the past. To bring the Gospel down to the tempo
of the jungle to make it popular is prostitution."

Memorial Church would be the laboratory where Ben
Cole would prove his point. We waited to see what would
happen!

Ben Cole began classes for young people meeting once a
week to build a choir that could sing the Gospel without
benefit of guitars, drums, mod outfits, and sideburns. With
his dedicated personality and musical ability he trained a
compact band from the best of the youngsters. A few teen-
agers went over to the Gospel Center, a fast-growing inter-
denominational church where a popular pulpiteer and a song
leader after the fashion of Chuck Robbins were packing them
in with programs geared to the latest trends in Gospel jazz.
It was a mixture from many church backgrounds. Almost
anybody could join and separation from the world was never
mentioned. Strange performers came from week to week, and
crowds flocked to it as to a theatre.

I began to preach on great doctrines of the church, and
Ben Cole worked with the kids. God honored His Word and
added to the church in genuine conversions. The excitement
of the revival had settled to steady progress. We were determined that it should mean something to be a church member, and we screened the prospects. Some who came by letter
from other churches did not like it when we enquired into
their past Christian experience. We felt that there should be
some evidence of having been born again. Bible standards of

Christian living were taught and discipline was instituted for those who needed it. This had not been heard of in a generation, of course, and some left in high dudgeon to join some church where they could live as they pleased.

Ben Cole and I sat up late many a night pondering the future of the church and Christianity. How the whole subject needs rethinking! How we need to get away from magazines, panel discussions, symposiums (where we pool our ignorance!) and read the New Testament as if for the first time! If one does that and views the times in the light of the Bible, one thing becomes clear: no church can be prosperous and popular and so-called progressive without conformity to the world, the flesh, and the devil. There can be no peaceful coexistence with this age. There can be no agreement between light and darkness, Christ and Belial.

Ben and I agreed that a New Testament Christian or church in these days will be radical and revolutionary in the eyes of men, and the object of their scorn and ridicule. There can be *not peace but a sword.* The wrong crowd—the liberals, the lawless, the anarchists—are getting the publicity as revolutionaries. The true revolutionary was Jesus Christ and the true church is "a persecuted minority, scorning the values of this world and living by stringent discipline." Old-fashioned New Testament Christianity is the very opposite of present-day fanatics, hippies, Communists, crackpots, and screwballs. Anybody who can *discern the times* in the light of Bible prophecy can find an explanation for any issue now in the headlines and what Christians should do about them. A generation stood between Ben Cole and me—but there was no gap in our understanding of the Church.

Memorial Church meant different things to different people. Some called it, "a fundamental bastion of exclusive orthodoxy." Others went to the opposite extreme and called us a band of fanatics on discipleship, attempting the impossible in such a world as we now have. So (depending on who was talking) we either froze or fried! But we were the talk of the town, pro or con—and why not? Taking Jesus Christ seriously is exciting business and makes news one way or another without trying to. If it *tries* to make news, it is not New Testament Christianity.

Soon Ben Cole's work with young people began to be felt outside the walls of Memorial Church. "Those smart-alec kids from Memorial," they were called in some circles. It started when Buddy Halleck disagreed with his science teacher about evolution.

The professor sarcastically commented, "It's been a long time since the Scopes Trial and I thought the disciples of William Jennings Bryan had all passed on."

That brought a laugh, but Buddy replied, "It's a strange time when Clarence Darrow, an agnostic, is lionized and Mr. Bryan, a Christian, is lampooned." (He had heard that in one of our classes.)

Then Jack Crawford repeated in history class something else from our class about "history within history"—God's history within human history, and that this is what really matters. His professor stared with uncomprehending disdain while Jack amplified his remarks by saying that there are two histories that run parallel, and that only in the Bible do we have God's outline of history. Of course it sounded smart-alecky, but are we to sit in silence while men advance their theories, and we have the only Book that has the true answers?

A third incident added fuel to the flame when Perry Huddleston refused to play with the high-school band at the Junior-Senior Prom. It was a matter of Christian principle as he saw it, and he lost his place in the band. He was not self-righteous about it. It gave him a chance to give a positive testimony and not pose as a *don'ter*.

Howson Lott, the realtor, owned some land east of Riverby. A beer company offered him a fine price for it as a brewery site, but he turned it down promptly. Lawton Mitchell who was on the city council opposed inviting the brewing industry to build a big plant in town. He lost, but he showed his colors while Richard Wilkerson, representative to congress and a prominent churchman in Riverby, approved the idea. The dividing sword was really flashing in all directions!

Helen Page was invited to take a leading part in a musical production in the City Auditorium. It was not rock music, but it was not the sort Helen had decided to sing for the rest of her life. She had already settled that issue with Bruce Lockerbie. There was considerable head-shaking among her former social circle. Some weeks later she sang in Memorial Church to a full house while Ben Cole and his youth choir gave a great program. While they furnished the background, Helen sang (as only she could), "Majestic Sweetness Sits Enthroned." Anyone who heard that without emotion must long since have had his heart petrified. When I looked about me at tear-filled eyes, I took heart. When our souls hunger for bread like this, why do some still feed us with stones?

Ben Cole had proved his case. In the closing hours of this doomed age there is no time for less than the best. Many ungracious things were being said—even by some ministers —about what had been going on in Memorial Church for months past. But that night when the congregation filed out, it was evident that the breath of heaven had silenced for at least that hour the mouths of the scorners. Late that night, one of the Riverby pastors called me to say, "If that is a sample of what is happening at Memorial, more power to you. I haven't felt like this since I used to go to camp meeting and hear a throng gathered under the arbor sing—and I've been singing it here in my study."

> No mortal can with Him compare,
> Among the sons of men;
> Fairer is He than all the fair
> That fill the heavenly train."

16
REVELATION AND THE FORTY-FOOT POLE

I began on Sunday nights in Memorial Church a series of messages on the Book of Revelation. Some of my fellow preachers considered Revelation a book of puzzles which they wouldn't touch with a forty-foot pole. But the people came as we moved into it, and we enjoyed the blessing promised to all who read *and keep the things written therein* (Revelation 1:3). We found that the strange and shadowy figures that move through its pages are not weird monsters in an apocalyptic riddle, but meaningful symbols unlocking the mysteries of our times.

The ignorance of the average man concerning the meaning of these days is appalling—but how can he understand them when all he knows is what he reads in papers and magazines and hears from television news commentators? Once we realize that we are the midst of a great warfare between God and the devil, now intensified because Satan knows that his time is short; when we discover that we are not wrestling flesh and blood, but are again reminded that we are *up against the unseen power that controls this dark world, and spiritual agents from the very headquarters of evil,* (Ephesians 6:12, PHILLIPS), then things make sense and current events fall into a design never dreamed of by newspaper editors and politicians.

For example: the anarchy, the riots, the violence, the looting and burning, the campus rebellion—all of this is part of the lawlessness our Lord predicted would precede His return (Matthew 24) and which Paul tells us will head up under Antichrist (2 Thessalonians 2:7-10). It has its roots in departure from authority in the Scriptures—in the home and in personal living. The campus disorders are simply the consequences of parental neglect and permissiveness along with the stupid philosophy of education popular in the last half century. We sowed the wind and we reap the whirlwind. Some of this generation of youth have had too much of everything except discipline, some have never learned to work, and know not the value of a dollar; now these erupt like spoiled brats throwing tantrums to get what they want. If they are smart enough to run the colleges, one wonders why they are in school. In an age that permits many youngsters to make their own decisions before they are even teenagers (for fear of frustrating Junior!), we need not be surprised.

Such preaching, of course, did not please some indulgent dads and moms who reminded me that I had no family of my own. A preacher's authority rests first, not in his experience, but in the Word of God and I had plenty of that!

To say all this does not enhance a preacher's popularity these days, especially when many of his fellow churchmen with their eschatology all awry are trying to bring in the brotherhood of man instead of looking for the Lord to return to set up His Kingdom. It is anathema to all the pulpit socialists who are traveling the same path that has led other religious bodies to spiritual decay. The insidious strategy that preaches tolerance (one-way tolerance if you're going their way!), subtly worms its way into places of authority, deceives gullible souls who do not know what time it is, infiltrates denominations, and builds the world church headed for Antichrist. This is Satan's masterpiece as an angel of light.

The Book of Revelation, rightly understood, exposes all these maneuvers—and maybe that is why it is so unpopular and neglected in some quarters. There is considerable wincing and squirming under such bright light—just as creeping and crawling things scatter when a rock is overturned and the sunlight strikes them. I observed some of this commotion Sunday nights and the flashing sword was much in evidence. Some hated the light and did not come to it lest their deeds should be reproved, but all who were doing truth came to the light that their deeds might be *made manifest, that they are wrought in God* (John 3:20,21). He who preaches Revelation may expect *not peace but a sword.*

17
DRILLING FOR SPIRITUAL OIL

I would not wish to create the impression that Memorial Church was only a storm center of controversy. The difficulties were only ripples along the riverbank and not the main stream. But the ripples indicate that the stream is going somewhere and that it is not a stagnant pond!

I had been concerned for some time lest the conflicts we had been passing through (as individuals and as a church) might sidetrack us into secondary issues and get us away from the centrality of our Lord. This can be a clever device of Satan to wear us out in incidental matters and make us lose sight of Him. It was a great blessing when Gideon Jones came to us for a week of Bible studies. He did not deal with current issues or prophecy. He majored on the Lord Himself and how our fulfillment is found only in Him by whom all things consist. How restful it was and how refreshing! How he made us see what untouched resources we had in our Lord!

One of his illustrations I will never forget. He told of a man who spent his life eking out a poor existence for years on a little farm. After he died, oil was discovered under his house! He had untouched wealth within reach, but he never knew what he had. He had it—and yet he didn't have it! All things are ours in Christ, but it is not what we have but what we

know we have that counts. And we must not only have it
(and know we have it) we must tap our resources just as the
oil must be tapped. We must lay hold upon what is already
ours.

Somehow this simple truth wrought wonders in my experience. Gideon Jones pointed out that many take Christ as
Saviour who never make Him Lord, and fewer still press on
to find that He is our Life. Of course these are not three
grades of Christian experience to be taken one at a time. We
do not take Christ *for* this or that or *as* this or that. We
simply take Him—*period*—for all that He is, but experience
deepens as we appropriate all we have in Him. Gideon Jones
liked to spell F—A—I—T—H as an acrostic: FOR ALL I
TAKE HIM.

Many were blessed by this week with our visiting brother.
Howson Lott is certainly not the mystic type, but he said to
me, "Preacher, I'm drilling my oil well!"

Gideon Jones made a suggestion that put us greatly in his
debt. He said, "The mid-week prayer meeting is the ther-
mometer of a church. You can tell what the spiritual temper-
ature is by Wednesday night. Everybody comes on Sunday
morning, but the middle of the week shows who is who.
Nowadays when what used to be the Lord's Day has become
the week-end, and the holy day is now a holiday, we may
have to make more than we ever did of the midweek service.
Why don't you have a family gathering to sing and testify
and pray with a message magnifying our Lord?"

We set out to do just that, and the service became known
to some as "the Jesus Meeting" for we sought to keep Him
at the center. We sang familiar hymns, let the people give
testimony to what Christ meant to them, then I gave a short
message, and we spent much time in serious prayer. Movies
were not necessary, and we did not have to think up some

new stunt or attraction each week. Christ was the attraction, and as we lifted Him up we felt His drawing power.

Right about this time the State Youth Conference was held in Riverby. As a matter of courtesy, I was asked to speak. I am sure that some of the leaders did not share my views, but they could hardly ignore Memorial Church. As I listened to some of the addresses, I did not wonder that our church youth are confused. The thrust was, of course, couched in terms of *relevance, involvements, dialogue, do your thing, happening* and all the new jargon. A new variety of Christianity was clearly among us!

My message was followed by a question-and-answer period. The same stock questions were asked, but I did not supply the usual answers heard these days. Some of the questions betrayed hostility to our position by the very tone of the inquiry. My own young people were there, and it was evident that Billy Burns and Ben Cole had not labored in vain. They gave a good account of themselves, but of course they were a minority.

At the end of the discussion, John Kincaid stood up. He was a ministerial student in college with a keen mind and dedicated heart. He was no convert of the new school.

"I notice," he began, "that most of your questions are the same you hear in every youth meeting. *What's wrong with this?* and *What's wrong with that?* The whole pitch seems to be, *How worldly can I be and still be a Christian? How near the precipice can I walk without falling off?* Why doesn't somebody ask, *How much like Christ can I be and how little like the world?* The whole approach is wrong—you are off on the wrong foot. People who are out to really follow Jesus Christ aren't forever asking, *Why can't I dance or smoke or play rock music?* It's about time we became positive instead of negative and majored on what we can do instead of arguing about what we shouldn't do."

That set a perfect stage for Ben Cole when he brought the closing address of the session.

"Militant and radical youth groups", he declared, "are out not to *do* but to *undo*. They would destroy the existing order, but they have nothing to offer in its place. Their reforms are politically and sociologically oriented; they do not sound like overflow of spiritual revival. The Wesleyan Revival produced great social changes as a by-product—the fruit of spiritual awakening. We are trying to produce the results without the cause. This is mere human reform, engineered by men in the energy of the flesh and it will come to nought. When we abide in Christ we abound, we bear fruit. The agitation today with its violence, bitterness, and hatred bears no marks of a movement of God, but of the devil, for it is rooted in Antichrist. A band of genuinely converted and Spirit-filled young people, yielded to the Lordship of Jesus Christ and witnessing by life and lip to Him could shake the world, and all the social benefits some are championing so loudly would follow as secondary benefits." (*That* rocked the conference!)

The next day things went pretty well as planned by the planners, but we had spoken our piece and borne our witness. It was easy to trace the pattern and strategy of the subtle movement that has undermined many another denomination and church. The same oily smoothness, mouthing Gospel terms when convenient, professing great love for Christ and boasting tolerance while intensely intolerant of opposition; so maneuvering as to make all of the old position appear un-Christlike and unloving and unsympathetic with human need. It made Memorial Chruch stand out like a sore thumb, but such is to be expected by all who choose *not peace but a sword.*

18
A LEAN BIRD IN THE WOODS

It had been many months since Stephen Lynn came to Riverby. The spiritual conflict is wearying, and I began to have physical reminders that I had better get away for some weeks "far from the madding crowd's ignoble strife." So I departed with Uncle Bill Blaine for his mountain cabin leaving Ben Cole to take care of everything. Uncle Bill was the best possible sort of companion for such a venture. I could relax with him, listen to his quaint philosophy—and his cooking was superb. He knew the woods and the birds. He never intruded. We could sit for hours and talk little or much as the mood struck us. Much of the time I spent on a favorite lookout on an uppermost crag. A lot of dust blows out of a man's soul in a spot like that!

In those two weeks I came to a new resolve: to give more time to meditation in solitude. I reflected on the ministers I knew. I had heard their complaints about how little time they had to be still. Caught in the ministerial rat race, slaves of a thousand parish demands that God never required in the first place—they break down. I am convinced that no man cracks up doing the will of God. He is our Father, not a taskmaster.

These preachers have their vacations, their golf, their hours of study and they try to pray, but none of these can take the place of meditation and reflection in the quiet place.

Our Lord spent much time there and set the example in the mountains or by the sea. I believe the preacher must find time and place for it at all costs, for the preacher who is available all the time is not worth much at any time.

I resolved to give one day a week to such solitude. I could not go to the mountain retreat every week, but I found a spot near Riverby. A preacher works on Sunday so he is still due a day of rest. I made it Saturday instead of the usual Monday so that I would be refreshed for preaching on Sunday. Of course, some dear souls would shake their heads at my disappearance every week, but they would shake their heads anyway, so it might as well be over something important. It meant declining a lot of worthless little meetings, but any man who would be a prophet must make up his mind early to say a courteous *no* to all invitations from the Sons and Daughters of I-Will-Arise.

The outdoors played a big part in the life of Bible prophets. Even Paul, who was a city man, prepared his theology in the deserts of Arabia. I am convinced that many of our distempers would vanish if we could escape outdoors. I am sure that the devil has no more effective device for crippling preachers than to tie them up as Delilah did Samson with a thousand little duties until they are reduced as Samson was to a treadmill, and the Spirit of the Lord has departed. This binding, blinding, grinding business may be executed by nice church people with the best of intentions and the worst of ideas about what a preacher is supposed to be and do. Instead of cords they may use dainty ribbons, but Samson is as powerless as if bound with chains. I remembered F.W. Boreham's description of a promising young preacher who started out a young giant but was so shackled by what he learned at seminary that he ended up "like a lion in curlpapers."

Some of my fellow preachers and some of my parishioners made remarks about my "Saturday in the woods." Some of them were probably jealous, and others grumbled because they could not control my habits enough to make a harmless little dominie out of me. And I remembered Spurgeon: "I'd rather be a lean bird in the woods than a fat bird in a cage."

19
ALDERSGATE *vs* THE MAJESTIC THEATRE

When Stephen Lynn came to Riverby, Linwood Sanders was one of the first to attend his meetings. He came to my study every week or so.

"I became a Christian when I was a little boy," he explained. "I'd been brought up in a good home and knew about Jesus from childhood. I didn't wander into great wickedness and had no vile past to repent of. It was a simple trust and there was nothing dramatic about my conversion. I'm glad I had a Christian home, but I've known all these truths from the start and I've sometimes wished I had never read the Gospel of John so that I could read it for the first time! I'd rather have a deep vivid experience of Jesus Christ than anything else in the world. Familiarity has not bred contempt, but it has bred complacency, I fear. I wish I could have the fresh and flaming experience of a brand-new Christian who has discovered all this for the first time. I'm living on dry faith and I need something to spark what I know and set it on fire."

He couldn't understand why—if he really believed all he said he believed,—if God had really come into the world to live as a man, if Jesus had died for our sins and had risen from the dead and was coming back again, Linwood Sanders couldn't understand why he wasn't more excited about it. Had he heard it too long or too much? It was too much like a fairy tale,—lovely to read about but somehow he couldn't translate it into the language of daily experience.

Of course, plenty of people are like that but few will admit it and some think that there is no more to be had. But when a man feels as Linwood Sanders did about it, something will happen. To him, however, it did not come as a vision or an inward ecstasy. He could not work up a subjective experience to suit him. One day, though, he came to see me radiant and rejoicing. He had been reading John 14:21: *He that hath my commandments, and keepeth them, he it is that loveth me: and he that loveth me shall be loved of my Father,* and *I will love him, and will manifest myself to him.*

He said, "I am putting this verse beside another from John: *And this is his commandment, That we should believe on the name of His Son Jesus Christ, and love one another, as he gave us commandment*" (1 John 3:23). Linwood went on. "I'm standing on First Peter 1:8: *Whom having not seen, ye love; in whom, though now ye see him not, yet believing, ye rejoice with joy unspeakable and full of glory.*"

Somehow Linwood Sanders had been converted and had become as a little child. The factual had become actual. It was as though he were a brand-new Christian. "I don't have any word for it," he said. "Call it assurance, witness of the Spirit, renewal—what you will. I suppose it could be taken apart psychologically. All I can say is that what I have known all along has come to life."

I thought of John Wesley—sincere, earnest, an Oxford man, of godly parentage—a man of prayer and a missionary, but not yet ready to preach. Whatever happened at Aldersgate made the difference. Linwood Sanders had his Aldersgate. How many thousands of our church folk have never come to theirs!

Once in a while books and movies make an effort to reproduce the life of Christ. It would be a great day for the church if we took it seriously enough to really live as though it actually happened. Familiarity with the language of Christianity from childhood has its dangers: it can be a substitute for the life itself. Too often we have the sickening feeling at church on Sunday morning that it is too much like a play. We commemorate it, but we do not duplicate it. We leave church with a comfortable satisfaction at having attended a performance, but with no thought of living all next week as though it happened once and can happen again. For Linwood Sanders, Jesus Christ lives today. It may have made some dear souls uncomfortable—those for whom the Gospel is cake for Sunday and not bread for every day of the week. He had discovered that the greatest adventure in this world is to bring Jesus Christ up to date by letting Him live again in us.

When we began insisting on the absolute Lordship of Jesus Christ at Memorial Church, it was interesting to watch the reaction and, in some cases, rebellion. Our people, like most church congregations, had been brought up to believe that "accepting Christ as Saviour" was all that was necessary in order to become a Christian. Submitting to Him as Lord was never thought of as part of the experience. That was called dedication, or surrender, something that usually came later —if at all—and if it never came, one would be saved anyway. Salvation is free, but along with it goes discipleship and that costs all we are and have. Plenty of church members will accept the free part but not the part that costs. So we have a come-in-Saviour—stay-out-Lord Christian who regards salvation as a cafeteria line where he can take what he wants and leave the rest. Therefore we have joiners aplenty but few followers.

I tried to make it clear that nobody could be a Christian who refused to make Christ his Lord as well as Saviour. Some called it theological hair-splitting. Some said we were mixing works with grace. Plenty of church members who say they have come to Jesus as believers refuse to come after Him as followers and resent any insistence upon His Lordship. I was appalled at the preponderance of church members who have merely professed faith in Christ, but who have no thought of letting Him govern their lives. This total misunderstanding of what it means to be a Christian has existed so long that to preach making Christ Lord as part of conversion sounds like some strange new doctrine. Comfortable church members who do not want their complacency disturbed rise up in revolt when told that unless they confess Jesus as Lord, they cannot be saved by merely accepting Him as Saviour. So we have a cheap Christianity that makes no demands for total allegiance to Christ as Lord. Our Lord could have had a multitude of cheap disciples, but always made discipleship costly and often lost His crowd.

I was prepared to preach some prospects away. We made it clear that we were not interested in building up a big membership of believers who refuse to be disciples. If some insisted on the free part, but refused the costly part they could go to other churches in Riverby where they could become church members without any change either outward or inward. Some of them did just that, accusing us of setting up arbitrary and impossible standards.

When Fred Forbush came to Riverby to become manager

of the Majestic Threatre, I learned that he and his family might join our church. It was just good business as far as Fred was concerned. Memorial Church looked big and imposing and he supposed that the *in* crowd belonged there. He could have joined without any questions asked in time past, but he did not know the story of what had happened to us lately. I would have received him and his family without batting an eyelash in those earlier days, but I had to go to his home to discuss with the Forbushes what it really meant to be a Christian. They looked at me as blankly as if I had been speaking in Arabic. But enough of it got through to make it clear that they were not ready for the kind of church we now were endeavoring to be. They appeared bewildered at not being welcomed with open arms as they had been elsewhere.

Curiosity as to what new kind of church this must be led to inquiries on their part. The new theater manager asked some of his civic club, his wife brought up the subject at the bridge club, and the two teen-agers brought it up with some of their classmates. The answers they got would make interesting reading. A few of our dedicated fellowship got in on some of the inquiries and for the first time in the lives of the Forbushes in and out of churches where they had lived, the light began faintly to dawn that being a Christian wasn't at all what they had supposed. Strange that after twenty centuries of Christianity the real thing is still news to multitudes of its professed adherents!

The Forbushes heard both sides, of course, and were not ready to pay the price of really doing business with Jesus Christ. They weren't looking for Aldersgate—they had the Majestic Theatre.

Would it not be better to refuse church membership to all

such than to get them in on the grounds that they can be converted later? The church is a nursery for babes *in Christ* but not a hatchery with the idea of taking in bad eggs in the hope that they hatch out into real Christians later. As it is, I could have led many people to Christ—if only they hadn't joined church first.

20
ADVISING JERRY CAMP

Jerry Camp came to me to talk about his future ministry. He was doing well in his pastorate, but he had done no graduate work and thought he had better get an extra degree if he expected to move on to a larger church.

"You know how it is," he explained. "Preachers are practically superannuated by the time they are forty-five if they have not reached an upper-bracket field by then. I feel sometimes that I should get out in the woods with my Bible and get a new message and a fresh anointing, but the church set-up today gives little credit to that sort of experience. God gives accreditation for it, but the brethren who operate clearinghouses for prospective pastors and flocks without shepherds don't pay much attention to John the Baptist fresh from the wilderness or Amos right out of Tekoah."

I didn't know how to advise Jerry. God has a habit of upsetting our well-laid schemes for making preachers. Jerry's reference to accreditation reminded me of Stanley Barlow, pastor of a great people's church. Crowds go there to hear old-fashioned singing and preaching. Stanley Barlow is a plain but powerful preacher. He graduated from a small Bible school that has no scholastic accreditation. He could never meet the requirements of a modern church looking for a pastor. Yet his congregation is larger than most of the modern churches!

One day he reflected on the whole business of accreditation. Said he: "Some say the church may go underground and be a despised sect in the last days as it was in the first days. We may have to forget about all kinds of accreditation from this old world—educational, social, religious, and every other sort. We may have to make our way without the credits and honors and degrees and status this age offers and go to Jesus without the camp bearing His reproach. I'm afraid we love the accreditation of men in all fields more than the praise of God. A lot of prophets through history didn't wear any decorations from the schools of men. They followed One of whom men said, *How knoweth this man letters, having never learned?*"

What lies ahead for young preachers I would not dare to predict. As the world church grows in these last days ministers may have to follow prescribed courses of training dictated from Headquarters or no pastorate (if we have pastorates then) will be available. It will be part of the faceless regimentation of all mankind readying them for the mark of the Beast. A few discerning spirits see it coming and the prospect is not pleasant.

The seven thousand who have not bowed to Baal will find a way, and God will still call prophets who bear no earthly credentials but whose commissions will bear the stamp of the Heavenly Headquarters. Maybe Jerry Camp ought to head for the woods after all! God's accreditation recognizes a curriculum quite different from ours. It is going to take sanctified grit to stand up to the pressures of Babylon in these perilous times.

21
HAVE YOU BEEN BORN AGAIN?

We began to emphasize at Memorial Church three questions: Have you been born again? Is Jesus your Lord? Have you been filled with the Spirit? We put them on our church folders. It is amazing how church people who have been let alone so long and not disturbed from the pulpit react when such pointed questions are asked: they resent them as intrusions into their private and personal affairs. So long have people been received into church with no questions asked, received almost hurriedly because we are so anxious to build up a big membership, that now any attempt to make it really mean something seems an impertinent interruption of the normal which is really subnormal.

All who are uncertain about their conversion dislike being faced with the question, "Have you been born again?" Some say that Jesus used that term only with Nicodemus and that it should not be made a standard test of Christian experience. The second question, "Is Jesus your Lord?" is unpleasant for those who are trying to get to heaven on Saviourhood alone, accepting the free gift but refusing discipleship. And as for the third, "Have you been filled with the Spirit?" that is considered a highly controversial subject and best left alone. Because of excesses on the subject, most people shy away from it altogether. Nevertheless, we continued to press those

three great questions and God honored it with some remarkable victories. I remembered reading how in one of the great
Revivals, a missionary visiting a certain field would station
herself at the door as the congregation went out and ask
every one, "Have you been born again?" I could not quite
bring myself to do that after church on Sunday morning and
yet I wonder why.

If all this is as serious as we say it is, isn't it important
enough to bring to the attention of every soul knowing that
any one of them might be in eternity before tomorrow? We
believe that the old Adamic race is lost in sin and that God
started a new race with His Son, Jesus Christ. As many as
trust Him become sons of God, and the only way they can
get into that race is by being born into it. Nobody can take
out naturalization papers and join it. If everything, being lost
or saved, hell or heaven, depends on that new birth, it is the
most important business on earth. Why are we so bashful
about it, so reluctant to bring up the subject with the once-
born men and women we meet every day? It just isn't done
except by a few brash souls who embarrass us by tackling
people head-on.

Linwood Sanders did it after his new experience which I
have already related. Sometimes when walking together we
met a "prospect" and Linwood would face him with "Have
you been born again?" I suppose my background and training just didn't develop that sort of approach, and Linwood
made me a little nervous. But if it is as important as I have
been preaching that it is, why do I wince when somebody
really acts as if it were that important? D. L. Moody dared
to do it in his early years as a soul winner. He may have
modified his approach with the passing years, but at the start
he certainly went about it as though everything depended on

it—and it does! Uncle John Vassar did it in Boston. On the other hand, some fanatics and crackpots do it, and that frightens us away from it.

If we knew for certain of impending disaster and others did not, we would feel no hesitancy in warning them. If the doom of the impenitent is as fearful as our Bible says it is, it is amazing that we keep tight-lipped about it even among good friends. It looks like we had better bring our behavior into keeping with our theology or take down our sign!

22
THE FALL MEETING AND THE ESTABLISHMENT

It was the annual fall meeting of our area churches where we heard reports of "the kingdom work" and what progress, if any, we were making. I had attended enough of these conclaves to feel little exciting anticipation. There were reports after reports droned out in dull, languid uniformity, and each one seemed to get a little duller than the one before. By noon I was exhausted, and had to take a walk in the woods to get my soul restored. The afternoon session held no promise of better things. One brother even added an appendix to his unusually long recital, and I was in favor of an appendectomy without examination!

Then our state missionary arose and began to tell of his past year in an isolated, neglected part of the state where he had contended with malaria, mosquitoes, and moonshiners for many years. It was a simple account of drunkards saved, homes restored, little churches begun. There were some statistics, but the figures glowed with fire. This was not just a report. Our brother breathed the breath of life into that meeting and it became a living thing. Here was primitive New Testament Christianity all over again.

That morning one of our leaders had set up charts and placards across the platform advertising how many baptisms we had set for next year's goal, how much money to be

raised, how many new churches to be started. These were
goals, but our missionary that evening was giving us not
goals but results. A morning speaker had spent himself trying to stir up the jaded spirits of a sleepy crowd, but that
afternoon it was not missions but a missionary—what had
been abstract was clothed in flesh and blood. People are not
stirred by addresses on evangelism but an anointed evangelist
makes evangelism come alive. The Gospel begins with the
Word made flesh and it is propagated by living incarnations
in transformed men and women. Yet we spend time and
money and effort promoting missions instead of producing
missionaries, forgetting that every Christian is meant to be
an evangelist. That sleepy crowd was willing to give money
to pay somebody else to do it just as we pay church staffs to
perform, and then gather on Sunday to watch them do it. If
only spectators could become participants and the performance could become an experience!

That was exactly what we had set out to do at Memorial
Church, and when the breath of God began to blow on that
valley of dry bones it was noised abroad as something sensational. Christians and churches around acted as though they
were ready to say, "Of course it's in the New Testament, and
I suppose we ought to do it but you really don't intend to try
it, do you?"

I suppose we'll go on holding rallies and pep meetings and
drives trying to persuade half-hearted and indifferent Christians to give more money and step up their "church work,"
adding more to a membership that already numbers too
many of the kind most of them are. Promoters would in-
crease Gideon's thirty-two thousand to fifty thousand when
God would reduce it to three hundred. If we dismissed all the
cowards and careless and left only the committed, the ratio
would still be what it was in Gideon's day!

I used to think that if a radiant, triumphant Christian came along, everybody would gravitate toward him, appreciate his character, warm up to him in their loneliness of soul. I used to think that if a church really experienced revival and set out to walk as our Lord walked, people would flock to it. That delusion was shattered when my own Christian life took a new turn, and when Memorial Church became the center of a new surge of New Testament Christianity. Of course I should have remembered that my Lord lived a faultless life, and was the most winsome character who ever walked on earth—but His contemporaries crucified Him. I should have remembered His words: *If the world hate you, ye know that it hated me before it hated you. If ye were of the world, the world would love his own: but because ye are not of the world, but I have chosen you out of the world, therefore the world hateth you* (John 15:18,19).

It is strange that we have to be reminded of this or learn it through bitter experience. In the months that followed the coming of Stephen Lynn, many moved out into glad, victorious Christian living, abiding in Christ and abounding in good works. Many more were converted or brought to deeper dedication. Lives were changed, homes were changed, discipleship took on new meaning and witnesses for Christ made Him known all over Riverby in shop and office and school and every walk of life. But instead of praise and commendation, we were the target of bitter assault by entrenched evil. And—wonder of wonders—church people and some ministers who should have rallied to us—joined our foes. Of course, once again, I should have remembered that our Lord's worst enemies were the religious people of His day, men who read the Scriptures, went to God's house, prayed in public, held high moral standards, were tithers and sought to win others to righteousness.

Neither Dr. McBane nor anyone else at the Main Office had a good word for what had happened in Riverby. Again I remembered that a prominent churchman of Wesley's day said he could see no great work of God going on although it was happening right before his eyes. The great Rowland Hill spoke contemptuously of "Wesley and his lay lubbers, draymen and chimney sweepers". If a Rowland Hill could feel that way about as great a work of God as the Wesleyan Revival, need we be surprised that lesser movements fare no better?

Some who are more interested in promoting an institution than in revival are naturally afraid of any spiritual ferment that might upset the status quo; but there will always be an Establishment, and if one system goes another will come. If it is born of revival, it ought to be a better one. Why worry?

One thing is certain: when the Establishment reaches the point where the possibility of a spiritual upheaval is distasteful, then something is wrong with the Establishment. When comfortable churchmen, secure in their systems, do not welcome the mighty wind of the Spirit because it might disarrange some of their papers and plans—and create a new order in which they are not qualified to serve—then it is time for such a fresh breeze from heaven.

During a Los Angeles smog of unusual intensity, a meteorologist said, "Only a wind from elsewhere can dispel this condition." It will take a heavenly wind of hurricane proportions to clear up our fog today. One would not predict just what things will be blown away if that Heavenly Hurricane ever blows in! But the air will be cleaner and the visibility higher. We might have to gather up some pieces and rebuild our structures, but such a renewal is long overdue. Our experience at Memorial certainly underlined that!

23
SOME GENUINE CHRISTIANS AND HARGOOD EVANS

It is a thrill to watch genuine Christians who have taken Christ seriously grow in grace and in the knowledge of the Lord. All our difficulties, problems, opposition encountered at Memorial Church, were as nothing compared to the onward and upward progress of our Master's Minority who had resolved to take the way of *not peace but a sword.*

Lawton Mitchell moved straight ahead in spite of home problems. A Christian with no encouragement from his own household but rather opposition carries a load that only he and God understand. Then, because of some of his changes in his business, there were financial losses. God does not guarantee prosperity to all who follow the Saviour! The new notion among some that God wants every man to be a millionaire does not bear the light of Scripture. Lawton Mitchell had more problems after his conversion than he ever knew before. You do not sharpen an axe on a cake of butter—it takes a grindstone, and Lawton Mitchell was being whetted to a sharp edge.

Howson Lott was the kind of rugged Christian you would expect. Matter-of-fact, practical, used to the rough-and-tumble of buying and selling, he was not very elegant, but there was an uncanny keenness of judgment that stood him in good

stead sanctified for the Master's use. Nobody needs more
common sense than a Christian in these days when the gullible are so easily led astray and false teachers would deceive,
if possible, the very elect. We made Howson Lott a deacon
and his sound advice was invaluable.

Sam Bradley continued to exert a fine influence over his
business associates and led several to church and two to
Christ. He was another valuable deacon with all the New
Testament qualifications.

Helen Page was in demand from many places to sing in
churches, evangelistic meetings, conferences, and conven-
tions. She was soloist for me on many preaching engage-
ments and always knew what to sing and how to sing it. A
college invited her to join its music faculty, but she preferred
her own private classes which were increasing in number and
which afforded a fine opportunity for her Christian testimony. A girls' trio of young singers who had been led to
Christ by Helen herself was a welcome addition to our
church program.

Helen Page refused to dress like the world. She was always
neat and attractive, wearing the best of clothes, but absolutely refusing the extreme styles. She had more than one
set-to in the dress shop which she had patronized before her
dedication to Christ. And when some church folk argued,
"What matters is not your clothes but your heart," then
Helen replied, "But the world can't see your heart—it looks
at your clothes." She resurrected the old virtues of simplicity
and modesty, claiming that dress should not attract undue
attention either way, toward extremes in either direction.

Helen was unanswerable on this subject. She never made
a fuss about it, but her example was more eloquent than any
sermons I might have preached. Her friends knew that she

could afford the latest garb and knew perfectly well what the newest fashions were. She was so attractive she outshone most of her critics without trying. She simply went her way following her convictions, but still she stood out because most Christians dare not be different and many women wear a garb they wouldn't be caught dead in if it weren't the style. She did not make an issue of it, but had Scripture and conviction to back up her practice—if anybody raised the question. We could use more of her kind for the supply is limited!

When Hargood Evans came to Riverby to speak for a week at Centenary Church, some thought that a second Stephen Lynn was among us. Some undiscerning souls thought he was saying the same things in a different way. He made much of Christ, but dwelt at length on the failure of the church. Institutional Christianity was his prime target and according to him the time had come to get out of stuffy sanctuaries and just be Christians out in the world where the action is. Of course, as with all such teachers, there was much in his preaching that was true and well put. We shared with him his feeling about a lukewarm Laodiceanism, but we did not arrive with him at his conclusions. Some of my own people were a little confused and unable to distinguish the fine lines between truth and error.

No one denies that we are seeing today a *Christless Churchanity*. That is Laodicea—institutional Christianity with the Lord outside the door calling out those *anyones* who will hear His voice and open the door to Him. Rich, increased with goods and needing nothing, we know not our true condition. He calls on such a church to repent, to be zealous, boiling, instead of lukewarm and threatens to spew it from His mouth.

But the answer is not a *churchless Christianity*. Some way-out groups today tell us that they like Jesus but not the church. There are lay movements and extra-curricular organizations today that are not church related. They endeavor to convert people to Christ, but leave them unaffiliated with any local fellowship of Christians. We do not accept churchless Christianity. Christ is the Head of the church and the church is His body. We are not preaching the Head without the body or the body without the Head. A bodyless Head is as unscriptural as a headless body. Christ is the Groom and the church is His bride. We are married to Christ (Roman 7:4) and espoused to one husband (2 Corinthians 11:2). There is no marriage without bride and Groom!

Some got the idea that just because we differed at times with the Establishment (and occasionally did not agree with the system) that we did not recognize organized Christianity. There *must* be some sort of organization to carry on the work of the Lord. Many groups have started out in revolt against denominationalism and they ended by becoming merely another denomination! They had bright ideas about being a mere fellowship without ordinances or deacons or ordained ministry or choir or building. Some even refused to take up offerings and put a box at the door for any gifts to the Lord. Some belong only to the invisible church and are invisible themselves on Sunday at any church. It is the other extreme from churchanity, but because the church is an organism does not rule out organization.

So we made it plain that Memorial Church was not endorsing Hargood Evans. Some dear souls who disliked any local church responsibility flocked to him because he seemed to provide an escape from being faithful to any church anywhere. They were free to visit any church or go to no church.

If they had their way all churches would be closed and Christianity would be hard to locate and pinpoint. Pity a visitor to such a town trying to get his hands on such an ephemeral fellowship! Memorial Church—for all its faults and failings—would be at least visible, and could be found on a city map! Yes, we were accused of having our heads in the clouds but we still kept our feet on the ground.

It was our dream that Memorial Church should be a center, a base, a citadel for a fellowship of disciples who had set out to be Christians in dead earnest, taking Jesus seriously. Of course the ideal is one thing and the actuality is another. The vision we have in hours of contemplation sometimes bears scant resemblance to the way it works out in some lives. The way John Smith demonstrates it through the week is not always a reasonable facsimile of what I preached on Sunday. By the time my sermon gets through the listener's mind and is translated daily in terms of his own understanding and personality, the original is often barely discernible. But that was true even of the disciples of the Lord.

For instance, Red McGuire interprets the ideal through the medium of his own rugged make-up. Nobody would accuse Red of being a theologian, and his colorful ways of saying what he believes might shock demure souls brought up in church circles and taught in conventional religious vernacular. But Red could put some Bible professors to shame with his loyalty and zeal. He had experienced two miracles—regeneration and healing—and he did not need to read it out of a book. *He knew.* It was first-hand with Red. He went after prospects with a head-on approach—more like felonious assault than the tactful sparring more cultured soul-winners might practice! After he had brought a dozen men somewhat of his kind to Christ and into the church, we decided we like it better the way Red did it than the way some of his critics didn't do it!

But, more remarkable still, Red could be effective with some who were not of his kind. His boss, Horace Evans, was a college man, successful in business, living out in the suburbs. He was skeptical of Red's conversion at first, and kept a shrewd eye on this rough-and-tumble, muscular Christian. But time went on and Red grew in grace and Horace Evans grew in appreciation. One day he called Red into his office and for two hours they talked "mostly about religion," as Evans put it. It led to a promotion for Red, and Horace Evans came to Memorial Church often to check on whatever it was that turned out such characters.

So everything was not opposition and hardship, for the consequences of serious Christian discipleship work both ways. Sometimes God honors His servants with earthly success and recognition. We preached that all this was secondary, that what mattered was being faithful to Christ whatever that brought in its train.

> To know no gain nor loss,
> My sinful self my only shame,
> My glory all the cross.

That was the note we sought to sound. By earthly standards—for some it meant loss, for others gain. What mattered was identification with the cross regardless.

I like the story of the grandfather who often took his little grandson along on short trips. One day, when invited to go, the little fellow asked, "Where are you going?" The grandfather went on alone and, when he returned, explained to the youngster, "If you had really wanted to go with me, you wouldn't have asked, 'Where are you going?' Where I was going wouldn't have made any difference." So we sing:

> Anywhere with Jesus I can safely go;
> Anywhere He leads me in this world below.

Whether it leads to success or scorn, to wealth or to woe, makes no difference. The true disciple does not ask, "Lord, where are You going?"

24
DR. PETE AND SEED-CORN
CHRISTIANITY

Everybody enjoyed the play on words about young Dr. Pete Moss being an avid gardener. Even as a boy he liked to putter around with flowers. It was his father's hobby, and Pete took to it naturally. All through his medical training it was his relaxation. His green thumb stood him in good stead. Pete Moss and peat moss made a good combination.

His father had high hopes that young Dr. Pete would be a big successful physician—at least in Riverby if he did not go to greater fields. A Christian movement among college students brought the young medic to a confrontation with Christ and a deeper dedication. Out of it grew a resolve to be a medical missionary in some remote area. His parents were aghast, but all their protests availed nothing. He had set his face like a flint. He was not interested in government-sponsored social service projects. (Bill Blaine said once, "We have a Peace Corps that started when the angels sang over Bethlehem!") And when he decided to go to the farthest-back recesses of our mountains as a sort of country doctor to mountaineers, the chagrin of his family was complete. Dr. Pete had come to Memorial Church after things began happening there. He naturally gravitated to a place where at least some were taking Jesus Christ seriously. He stayed with us until he was ready to move deep into his mission field.

Of course there was the expected shaking of heads among the uncomprehending souls who know nothing of dying to live. I was reminded of the missionaries who started for Africa on a ship before the days of air travel. The ship's captain said, "You'll die in those jungles." One of the missionaries replied, "Captain, we died before we started!" So Dr. Moss had died before he started. Strange that after twenty centuries of Gospel preaching so few church folk seem to have heard about the corn of wheat falling into the ground and dying that it might bear much fruit! Of course the natural man, the once-born, can see no sense in it, but even professing Christians know little of God's seed corn and how we die to live—and go down to go up.

Memorial Church warmly supported Dr. Moss both with prayers and money. When he returned to tell of his work one Sunday night we had a demonstration of personalized Christianity. Missions in the abstract do not thrill or challenge, but a real live missionary clothes it in flesh and blood. It is a far cry from the comfortable Sunday morning church bench-warmer to seed-corn Christianity. One is like a package of garden seeds in a pretty Sunday morning display. The other is that package torn open and the seeds planted in the muddy ground. So little of packaged Christianity ever becomes planted Christianity! Dr. Pete was not interested in merely being one coin in God's collection. He would be God's spending money! I think a lot of people woke up that Sunday night to learn that we are all missionaries, but most of us are on furlough before ever going to the field!

Dr. Pete had not gone to the mountains merely to heal bodies but to save souls. He was concerned first with the mother disease, sin, and he represented the Great Physician.

Environmental pollution was secondary to moral and spiritual pollution. Learning how to read and how to do better farming were secondary to first becoming Christians. He was out to deal with the main trouble, and he followed his Lord's pattern of preaching, teaching, and healing. His medical skill and his green thumb were powerful assets, but he would not let the good defeat the best.

When I grow weary of the rat race and so much meaningless religious activism, I take a trip to Dr. Pete's station back of beyond—and get a refresher course in primitive Christianity. For this is how it started.

25
WHAT YOU HAVE IS A HUMBUG

Most people in Riverby thought it was perfectly wonderful when it was advertised that there would be a United All-Faiths Religious Service one Sunday night in the Colosseum. Catholic priests, Jewish rabbis, and Protestant clergymen had all been invited, and it would be a glorious expression of unity among all faiths. To hear Dr. Maitland of Centenary Church tell it, you would think the millenium was about to break upon us. But Uncle Bill Blaine was leery of such strange combinations, and remarked that if you put together the head of one bug, the body of another, the wings of another, and the legs of still another—what you have is a humbug.

When I announced that services in Memorial Church would be held that night as usual, the response over town was less than enthusiastic. The *Record* carried an editorial lamenting the fact that any church could dream of doing aught but cooperating when religious faith is on the decline, when God is pronounced dead in some quarters, and the church is fast losing its grip upon mankind. At the ministers' meeting I tried to make my position clear in substantially these words:

"We are glad to cooperate with all citizens on a civic basis to support any worthy community cause and work for any

improvement of a social nature. But to share the platform
with diverse groups who deny what we affirm in spiritual
matters is to be untrue to our convictions and extremely
confusing to the general public. The man on the street as-
sumes that when we all come together in this fashion our
differences really do not matter much. Everything is reduced
to one common denominator in a sort of general religion. We
believe that an individual Catholic—if he has personal faith
in Christ—is a Christian in spite of the accumulated tradi-
tion and false doctrine which his church holds, but the system itself is another matter, and we cannot lend any public
support to Catholicism as a system. We are glad to cooperate
with our Jewish friends in any common enterprise for better
conditions, but to join in a service of religion is construed by
the average observer as a sort of endorsement of a faith which
repudiates Christianity because it does not recognize our
Lord. We do not believe alike, and I am not interested in
trying to present an image of unity which does not exist."

So cleverly does Satan the Mock Angel maneuver in the
ecumenical delusion that it seems downright un-Christian to
take no part in it. Against the background of such evil times
as these, certainly all good people should try to get together!
Nothing is thought important enough to hinder. So the modern Babylon shapes up and all grades and shades of religion
are dumped into one theological mulligan stew. We forget
that the early church grew not by consolidation, but by
diffusion. Mob-ilizing into one vast fellowship a throng of
people who know not what they believe adds no strength
except to error. One hundred blind men can't see any better
than one blind man!

There was plenty of head shaking in Riverby, and
Memorial Church got one more demerit as the erratic and

uncooperative odd number among the churches. There was not much use trying to explain. To those who do not understand, no explanation was possible; to those who do understand no explanation was necessary. It was just another lesson in *not peace but a sword*.

26
ALL CHRISTIANS ARE MISSIONARIES

Some of the men of Memorial Church, including Red McGuire, Howson Lott, Sam Bradley, Lawton Mitchell, Linwood Sanders, Ben Cole, and myself had a habit of eating supper together Thursdays at one of the cafeterias before we started out on a round of visitation. Others joined us, and we had an enjoyable time of prayer and fellowship before setting out on our rounds. We became a familiar sight at this eating place, and some jokingly called us The Holy Club with some reference to John Wesley's days, I suppose. Our young people had a similar band that met down at a pizza parlor once a week. They were quite a novelty to onlookers since they did not play the rock music but sang Gospel choruses instead. They were gay and full of life, but it was a different kind of happiness. It evoked criticism on the part of some, but it attracted others and their numbers grew. They carried New Testaments which led some wag to observe that they reminded him of the Chinese youth in the television news waving copies of the little red book of Mao-Tse-tung.

How strange that after twenty centuries a group of happy young Christians and a group of older laymen should be viewed with curiosity because they got out of church walls with their testimony! Of course the reason is that all such is a departure from the usual normal (subnormal) concept of Christianity as limited to church on Sunday. Satan would like to keep it cooped up within four walls and restricted to a fixed routine. This breaking out into the stream of weekday life raised some eyebrows, but it should be the regular life of the church. It's true that we meet on Sundays at the base to prepare for our main business as we radiate out in all directions where we live and work. These forays of the laymen and youth are not meant to take care of our Christian responsibility all week. They are special activities, but we are meant to work at it in office and shop and school and wherever we are all week. I worked hard trying to get across the point that we are all in full-time Christian service instead of limiting that term to preachers and missionaries and all who draw a salary for doing church work.

I found that these two teams along with Helen Page's group and others brought to church on Sunday prospects, not merely for church membership, but for Christ. They had already been witnessed to and dealt with, not merely invited to church. When I gave the invitation these workers brought their friends down the aisle. They had already been conditioned and readied, and I had little to do. All my life I had heard what would happen if "one won one" and that one won another until soon the church was filled, but I had never seen any church really do it. It was usually left to the pastor and some of the staff while the members came on Sunday to see who the pastor and staff had won all week. This I considered a perversion of Christianity, and it was made plain that all Christians are missionaries and are not spectators and onlookers on Sunday.

It is amazing how few church members ever suspect that they are supposed to be involved in anything more than church attendance and financial support of the budget! It all goes back to the fact that so few have had a personal experience of Jesus Christ or are following Him seriously. There is no use trying to drum up a love for Christ and souls that is not in the heart. Sending out a band like that whose own hearts have not been touched will do more harm than good. Too much damage has been done by church teams out on a dull assignment to get more members. This is for burning hearts who have met the Master and are walking with Him day by day.

27
SPECIAL TARGETS: THE MASTER'S MINORITY

Whoever holds the notion that most of our troubles are over when we begin Christian discipleship in earnest is in for a rude awakening. The Master's Minority at Memorial Church soon found themselves to be the special targets of the powers of darkness. Lawton Mitchell lived daily with the problems of a divided home. The tension did not lesson, but grew with the passing months. A man who must contend with the modern business world all week and then find no respite when he comes home needs an extra supply of grace. It either deepens a man's devotion or drives him to despair. Mitchell told me that he had underscored the seventh chapter of Micah. It describes conditions much like our own day, and states that in such a time a man may not even be able to talk things over with his own wife (v.5). But Lawton Mitchell had learned to live in the seventh verse: *Therefore I will look unto the Lord; I will wait for the God of my salvation: my God will hear me.*

Our dedicated young people faced problems with pagan youth in high school and college—to say nothing of some professors who scorned their views in history and other classes. Business and professional men discovered that all-out devotion to Christ made them conspicuous both because of things they did and things they did not. Sometimes it brought respect, sometimes reviling. In politics, low ethical standards made an honest Christian of conviction and character stand out by contrast. Such good men make evil men uncomfortable by their godly lives, and the discomfort grows into resentment and ridicule. When twice-born people try to make their way through a world run largely by once-born people, trouble is sure to come.

This bears repeating: How strange that after twenty centuries of Christianity a church that set out to really take Jesus seriously should be censured—not so much by the outside world as by other preachers and churches! I had a letter from an old college classmate of mine who had followed the course of events at Memorial during the past year.

"What have you gained," he asked, "above what you had when you followed the regular course and did not preach this stepped-up discipleship that has lost some of your best members and gotten others into plenty of trouble?"

I could only reply, "We are not a perfect church. There never has been a perfect church, even in the New Testament. We are sinners saved by grace with many faults and failings. We carry a treasure in earthen vessels. At least we are on the road and going somewhere. This is real spiritual conflict, not shadow boxing. Some churches are peaceful because the devil already has them where he wants them and does not disturb their rest. We are dealing with reality, undertaking to live out day by day what many merely commemorate on Sunday as though it were a legend. This is not a fairy tale, a storybook of happy endings; it is warfare with unseen foes, and we are not on a dress parade. It cannot be understood by all Reubenites who prefer the shepherd's flute to the battle trumpet—to all inhabitants of Meroz who come not to the help of the Lord against the mighty!"

28
LINWOOD SANDER'S WITNESS AND DR. MAITLAND'S "INVOLVEMENT"

I have already written about Linwood Sanders and how he came "not to a new lease on life, but to a lease on a new life" as he put it. One of our Christian writers, A. W. Tozer, has said: "Many of us Christians have been extremely skillful in arranging our lives so as to admit the truth of Christianity without being embarrassed by its implications."

Linwood had decided to live the Christian life—implications and all. He began in a manner that astonished even the Master's Minority of Memorial Church. I do not think the Lord expects us to follow Linwood's example literally. I could not, and he may have overdone it at times—but who am I to say?

A bachelor of simple tastes Linwood was a photographer and did excellent work in his mid-Riverby shop. He did not have strict hours, but his work was so good that people waited until they could find him in. Any customer was sure to hear a good word about Jesus Christ, not preachy but well-worded and *in season*. When he was out he was all over Riverby with his witnessing, speaking in churches and other places. Of course some thought he had gone off on religion. A generation like this would not understand a man who absolutely refused to get caught in the rat race—who had only pity for the go-getter, Madison Avenue, high-pressure salesman so busy gaining the world that he loses his own soul. The Lord made Linwood's business to prosper, but he gave away most of his earnings. He made his own schedule, reported to no main office. His Spartan simplicity must have been frustrating to tax collectors who found so little to list. He did not advocate vows of celibacy and poverty, but he must have been irritating to some status seekers. Of course he had good scriptural precedent in the Apostle Paul who had no family, made tents for a living, and had little of this world's goods. He sought only to lead men to Christ and did. He dealt almost entirely with men for he was wary of "silly women" with an eye on a prosperous bachelor. Linwood was a good antidote to many of us often beset with the cares of this life.

He sometime made the remark that four categories of people would not be numerous in heaven. He listed the rich, the wise, the mighty and the noble with Scripture to prove his point (Matthew 19:23,24; 1 Corinthians 1:26). He called them the plutocrats, the intelligentsia, the VIPs, and the bluebloods. This classification did not go over too well in some quarters, but nobody could contest it unless they wanted to challenge Paul and the Lord Himself. I felt that we needed a Linwood Sanders among us to offset our tendency to try to make the grade in one or the other of these four brackets.

How strange that after all these centuries of church history we still think a man strange if he gets along without so much we deem indispensable! There is no denying that our Lord and Paul traveled light through this world and Linwood Sanders followed in good succession. Our Lord's counsel to the rich young ruler and His general advice to His disciples hardly fit into the success textbooks of these times. If Linwood sometimes went a bit too far, it was mild error compared to our mad scramble for money, sophistication, power, and prestige. Any man who can buck such a tide today is a valuable member of any band of pilgrims headed heavenward.

To go across town, (both geographically and theologically), Dr. Maitland of Centenary Church did not share my views on involvement. He believed that we should fraternize and mix with the world in order to permeate, infiltrate, "leaven" it with our Christianity. He belonged to the country club and sipped ginger ale at the cocktail parties. He joined a procession of demonstrating protesters and got his name in the papers as identified with numerous reform projects. He was appointed to several important posts in civic circles. Like Lot he sat in the gate in Sodom. He reminded me, too, of Obadiah in Ahab's court, out looking for grass in a time of drought instead of praying with Elijah for showers of blessing.

I was reminded also of a word from F.B.Meyer, "There is not a single hero or saint whose name sparkles on the inspired page who moved the times from within." Archimedes thought he could move the world if only he had a point outside it where he could set his fulcrum. Lot did not have much leverage within Sodom nor did Obadiah in Samaria. As I have said before, we must go to our Lord without the camp bearing his reproach. Of course Obadiah hid a hundred prophets from the wrath of Jezebel, but a hundred prophets who must be hidden would probably be worth little in broad daylight. Christians who stand in with the powers that be may sometimes be helpful as was the Elector of Saxony in the days of Luther and John of Gaunt in the times of Wycliff. But as time went on it became evident that Dr. Maitland was not converting the circles he moved in, but was more like a woman who marries a drunkard to reform him. Indeed he was not remolding Riverby as much as Riverby was rubbing off on him!

It amazed me that Memorial Church should be accused of self-righteous isolation when actually her members were scattered all over Riverby throughout the week in their work and social contacts winning people to Christ. Howson Lott, Sam Bradley, Red McGuire, Linwood Sanders, and many more were continually reaching people who, when converted, in turn brought others so that several hundred new disciples were letting their light shine in all sorts of places. Helen Page continued to witness in music circles. Our young people made their presence felt in school. Peter Hobbs, although outnumbered, bore a good testimony in city council. Homes were changed, many a business felt the impact of changed lives, and all Riverby was made aware of a new force in town. Preachers and churches elsewhere heard of God's work among us. As with Thessalonica long ago, from Memorial Church sounded out the word of the Lord so that in many another place our faith was spread abroad.

What more is a church supposed to do anyway? Of course Dr. Maitland thought the millenium would be ushered in and the Kingdom set up by education, legislation, reformation, under religious auspices. His eschatology did not envisage the sudden return of our Lord at the close of an age ending in anarchy, apostasy, and apathy. We were out, not to Christianize but to evangelize our generation. God is taking out a people for His name and we would gather as many as we could.

Ignorance of God's program for these days and the substitution of a program of our own makes for untold confusion.

In Riverby it divided the professing church into two camps going in opposite directions. How bewildering to the man on the street trying to reconcile Centenary Church with Memorial!

29
SACRAMENTALISTS AND
SUPERSAINTS

I had been much concerned about the way we observe cur two church ordinances, baptism and the Lord's supper. Baptism has become merely a rite by which we join the church and has almost no significance for the average Christian. If he were called upon to state the meaning of it, the answers would be amazing. Certainly very few rise from the baptismal waters to walk in newness of life. Identification with Christ in His death and resurrection means nothing. I found that it paid off to take time before each baptismal service to explain the meaning of the ordinance. I had, of course, gone into it fully beforehand with the candidates. Regular sermons now and then setting forth the symbolism of both ordinances helped to screen out any who would join us for unworthy reasons. My own denomination has leaned over backward to escape sacramentarianism, and lest the ordinances come to mean too much, we have made them mean next to nothing.

We observed the Lord's supper on the first Sunday night of each month. Instead of a dry ritual, it came to be one of our most meaningful meetings and everybody looked forward to it. I found that I needed not fear that I would run out of suitable sermons for that occasion for the ramifications are boundless. While of course we did not hold to either transubstantiation or consubstantiation, we did try to rescue the Lord's supper in our church from an empty ceremony. It glows with meaning when we look back to our Lord's death and forward to His coming.

He also said, *Except ye eat the flesh of the Son of man and drink His blood, ye have no life in you.* The Lord's supper goes beyond a memorial to symbolize that we partake of the blessings of His death. It says also that Christ is not only our Saviour but our Sustenance, just as the Passover lamb was eaten after the blood was sprinkled on the door posts of the Israelites. Partaking of the bread and wine thus declares to the world that we live by the constant appropriation through faith of Christ who is our Life as well as our Lord. We partake unworthily when we fail to discern our Lord's body, the true meaning behind the symbols. When all this is understood by a congregation, the Lord's supper becomes a highlight of the month, and so it was at Memorial.

Of course, word went around among some of the brethren that we were making too much of the ordinances and becoming sacramentalists. Just let a little life begin to pulsate in a church and all resters-at-ease in Zion elsewhere begin to complain because their slumbers have been disturbed. Memorial Church in its preaching and practice attracted some and repelled some. We were often reminded of the early church when some dare not join the fellowship but believers were added to the Lord (Acts 5:13,14). People who meant business were drawn to us, and the superficial seeking only a status symbol went elsewhere.

After all, we were not out to add more members, to build up impressive statistics that would look good in the denominational annual and enhance my chances of promotion. We were out to win people to Christ and His church, believer-disciples who would trust Him as Saviour and obey Him as Lord. When that is made clear, it screens out mere joiners. Of course new members are not expected to be theologians nor to understand all that is involved, but there is a world of difference between honest and earnest Spirit-moved people and casual prospects.

We had grown accustomed to the jibes and sly remarks about Memorial Church being a Club of Supersaints. We had all kinds of Christians in the fellowship representing diverse grades and shades of spiritual experience. Some were babes in Christ, some were retarded, some were anemic, others were growing, going and glowing in abundant health. Some were not making the progress they should; some grew weary in well-doing. Delinquent members were dealt with and if they continued to show no evidence of interest and did not attend the meetings or contribute in any way to the work— after being given every opportunity to change their course— they were dropped from the membership. In this permissive age of mild tolerance, such procedure is almost unheard of and was of course censured. The average individual today has no discernment whatever in such matters and even the denominations boast of their inclusiveness with room enough for everybody.

It is one thing to deal with weak Christians but quite another to contend with outsiders who get into church without conversion—who do not believe or practice the things the church stands for. When Randall Pierce, a lawyer in Riverby, joined our church he gave assent to our standards and requirements but it soon became evident that he reserved the right to put his own interpretation on them. This clever device is the trick of all wolves who get among the sheep by employing the old terminology when it suits their purpose while they mean something entirely different. It is dishonesty of the lowest order and far below the infidel who plainly says what he believes or does not believe.

Randall Pierce soon became teacher of the Men's Bible Class before his true colors were evident. Before long we discovered that he was not one of us. His views on doctrine were an utter contradiction to ours and his stand on Christian conduct became an embarrassment. He built up a class with many outsiders not members of our church. Satan had deftly maneuvered this Trojan horse into our midst. We were faced with the prospect of the same fountain sending forth both bitter water and sweet. We began to hear the gossip that one could hear one kind of preaching from the Memorial pulpit and another from Pierce's Bible Class.

It was my unhappy lot to have a direct confrontation with Pierce, and then he was asked to appear before our deacons. Both times he was adamant. Finally it became necessary to dismiss him from teaching the class and drop him from church membership. The reverberations were felt all over Riverby. In a day like this such action is of course incomprehensible but we did not waste time trying to explain it. We said, "This too shall pass"—and marched straight ahead.

Our course had followed prayer, deliberation, and every effort to correct the offender. After that, to have gone on marking time would have spelled disaster. Theodore Roosevelt, as president, said he dug the Panama Canal first, then they debated it afterward. If it had been debated first there might not have been a canal. There are knots that cannot be untied, they can only be cut. There is no way to unravel some issues without getting unraveled yourself in the process. We survived, and Pierce went over to Centenary Church where everything goes, and he could deny the Scriptures and wrongly divide the Word to his heart's content.

30
NEW FIRES TO KINDLE

The preacher or church setting out to preach and practice New Testament Christianity in a day like this soon learns that there is a price to pay. If I had continued the course I pursued before Stephen Lynn came to Riverby, I could have enjoyed smooth sailing. Few crises would have arisen. I could have preached popular, pleasing sermons, belonged to the clubs, spoken to important church gatherings, been elected to top positions in the Establishment. To take an all-out stand for sound doctrine and dedicated living meant suspicion from the Establishment, criticism from the world —and, of course, prospects who merely wanted to join a church would go elsewhere.

Christianity is so meshed into the warp and woof of this age that there is no contrast, and average Christianity produces not even the lift of an eyebrow but only a yawn. Let any preacher, Christian, or church revert to and recover the New Testament pattern and there will be trouble. Dr. Maitland in one of his sermons, probably aimed as a left-handed swipe at what had been going on at Memorial Church, pointed out that Christians as the salt of the earth and the light of the world should be quiet, unobtrusive, creating no stir. But salt and light make a radical difference which is not very evident on the average scene today.

Although our ministry at Memorial Church brought opposition and criticism, it brought something else. Preachers
and churches had heard and read about what had been going
on among us. Some came to look on and study the movement. I was invited to other churches to tell about it. Calls
for weeks of special services began to come. It was not easy
to define just what our ministry would be. It would not be
evangelism or Bible teaching in the usual sense. *Revival* was
a term so misused that it had come to mean just a drive for
more church members. What I wanted to do was to gather
in every church a nucleus, an assembly of *anyones,* kindling
wood to start a fire, a Master's Minority, a church within the
church, just as had been done at Memorial. We are so accustomed to doing things the big way in church as everywhere
else that no American church leader would think of reducing
Gideon's army from thirty-two thousand to three hundred.
The promotion experts would try to raise it to at least fifty
thousand! The American mind finds it almost impossible to
think in such terms so not only are Gideon Bands a rarity,
but Gideons are scarce—and you must have a Gideon before
you have a Gideon's Band.

I began to feel an urge to make this my business. I knew
it meant no salary, an uncertain ministry that had no place
in the set-up today. I would have to make my own niche and
create my own category. My seminary comrades of other
days (many of whom already viewed me askance) would
write me off for good if I took to the road without the blessing
of headquarters and with no home office but heaven. But the
Master's sword not only cuts us off from evil, but sometimes
from things we hold dear. If we are to hate loved ones and
even our own lives, certainly we must be prepared to renounce a comfortable income and the security of a fixed and

recognized profession. I had faced *not peace but a sword* as
a pastor, now I must face it as a traveling preacher without
the customary portfolio. It would be as difficult to explain my
work as Amos found it in the Establishment at Bethel.

If ever a David had his Jonathan, I had mine in Ben
Cole. He had begun with us as a youth director, but he
quickly developed gifts that made him a splendid associ-
ate pastor. He was both old-fashioned and up-to-date, and
a rare specimen of youth with wisdom generally born of
age. We stood together and bridged the generation gap
with a challenge to both youth and adults.

I took a trip to the woods with Uncle Bill and there I
settled the matter of my future ministry. I would take to
the road to kindle elsewhere the fires begun at Memorial.
I would look to the Lord and His people for support. I
spent hours on my favorite lookout with my Bible. When
I returned and broke the news to the church there was a
stunned silence at first, but I knew that they would want
God's will to be done. Lawton Mitchell stated it best
when he said, "We are ready to share this ministry with
others, and our pastor will now become our missionary!"
They exacted from me the promise that I would return
once a year for a week of preaching.

The second move was to ask Ben Cole to take over as
interim pastor. That was changed speedily, and he was
called to be permanent pastor. As Sam Hadley put it,
"No other man could understand what has been going on
at Memorial. A new man, however well-intentioned,
would find it difficult to continue what has been begun,
for this is not an ordinary case of a church merely looking for a new pastor." I was overjoyed for I shuddered at
the prospect of some novice trying to get the church back

to the usual beaten path and revert to what it had been before Stephen Lynn came to Riverby.

For some days I had sinking spells about the choice I had made. I could pray, but I knew that many a day and night of loneliness lay ahead when Satan would tempt me to despair. I had encouraged myself with the example of Paul, but he had Silas and Barnabas and Luke.

Uncle Bill Blaine made no bones about it. "You need a wife", he said. "This hard old world is too much to tackle alone." He couldn't understand why I hadn't teamed up with Helen Page. "You go everywhere to preach and sing. Looks like the Lord has teamed you up anyway. Why don't you catch on?"

What Uncle Bill had not caught on to was that I had been in love with Helen Page for some time. I had admired her for her gifts and consecration. We had shared many meetings on preaching trips. Admiration had deepened into love—and I told her so. But she knew that I faced the call of my new ministry and that I had felt that I should undertake it alone. She understood the conflict, and said she would not want to complicate my problem. Then, too, she had been pondering whether she should go into Gospel music fulltime and therefore had somewhat the same problem. I needed wisdom and claimed it according to James 1:5. It is easier to write books about guidance than to get it sometimes, and we are always prone to rationalize what we want to do until we call it God's will—and find a convenient verse of Scripture to justify it. (When anybody as wonderful as Helen Page gets all tangled up in the problem a fellow had better get outside help!)

31
WHEN THREE IS NOT A CROWD

Light came from two directions. Dear Mr. Davies, the Welsh brother, counseled me. "Do not overdo this matter of the dividing sword," he advised. "Your tendency to asceticism and solitude can become a snare. *No good thing will He withold from them that walk uprightly. Delight thyself also in the Lord; and He shall give thee the desires of thine heart.* You need the steadying and corrective assistance of a likeminded companion. This is a lonely road you are taking and you will tend to magnify matters which a good helpmeet would reduce to their right size. I believe you both are prepared to *hate* all other attachments in the sense our Lord intended when He spoke about *not peace but a sword.* Your love for each other will be lost in your love for Him."

As the time drew near to begin my new work, most of the calls requested that Helen Page be the soloist and maybe conduct women's meetings!

It was early autumn and the week before I was to leave Riverby I drove alone to my retreat in the mountains. The afternoon spread before me in glorious stillness. A deep peace filled my heart. I had talked things over with Helen, especially the two leadings I have just mentioned. We prayed about it together, and I told her that it would be wonderful if she could give me her answer before I went away. We were to be in meetings together later, but I felt that I could not continue in an unsettled state for weeks to come.

The sun sank low and I turned to start homeward. I had been aware of the presence of the One Called Alongside to Help. He would not leave me nor forsake me. If He wanted me to go alone I would still not be alone. I started down the trail and there—more beautiful than I had ever seen her before—stood Helen. The light in her eyes was enough. She did not need to say anything. We stood on the crag and pledged ourselves to the Unseen Third Party in a lifelong tryst. Three is not a crowd at a time like that!

The path for many months past had been rough at times, and the test of the Dividing Sword had brought changes I never dreamed of when I came to Riverby. Some thought I had fouled up a fair future by well-meant extremism. I had passed through long hours of agonizing decisions. But all the agony was forgotten in the ecstasy of that autumn afternoon when Helen and I walked down that mountain trail together.

POSTLUDE

When I had finished this account, I took it over to Mr. Davies and read it to him one summer afternoon. "I am not an expert at this kind of writing," I said, "and it may displease more people than it pleases, but I think the story should be told."

"Go ahead with it," was the reassuring answer. "It ought to arouse some preachers and churches who are complacently satisfied with far less than they could be and do—who have settled for the good when they could have the best. On the other hand, it may help some who expect too much. There are no perfect preachers or churches and this is not the millenium. One day our Lord will present a faultless church, but in the meantime we must remember that Christians are people—we press on toward the prize. It will sound too preachy to some who rest at ease in Zion and not fiery enough for others with more zeal than knowledge—but it will bless all disciples who are committed to the Way that means *not peace but a sword.*"